THE NO-DRAMA MANAGER

—⁂—

PRAISE FOR *The No-Drama Manager*

The *No-Drama Manager* is a must-read for anyone who is or is about to be in a management position of any level in any type of organization.

It reminded me once again how easy it is to complicate the role of managing by trying to do what others are put in the position to do. I have seen first-hand how managing with Eldon's No-Drama method helps direct reports grow and become enthusiastic about their work. Using the commonsense approach to managing has given me the opportunity to make a difference in several corporations that needed new leadership. Thank you, Eldon, for the much-needed reminder.

—Chuck Bailey, President
Global Marketing Group

───⟜⟞───

I read Eldon Spady's book before I started my first management job, and I still use his principles every day. This book shows that you can be an effective leader by being clear, compassionate, focused, and level-headed. I am grateful to Spady for sharing wisdom that isn't just the flavor-of-the-month."

—Neil Chethik, Director
Carnegie Center
for Literacy &
Learning,Lexington, KY

THE
NO-DRAMA
MANAGER

*A Commonsense Approach to
Being a Better Manager*

⟨✦⟩

By Eldon N. Spady

CreateSpace

The No-Drama Manager

Copyright © 2012 Eldon Spady

Edited by Neil Chethik

Cover and interior design by RMcB Creative Services

ISBN 978-1470007225

LCCN 2012901974

Printed in U.S.A. by CreateSpace

✦ TABLE OF CONTENTS ✦

✦ ACKNOWLEDGMENTS ❦

I want to thank my wife Lorraine for her editing help and, along with her, my daughters Sonia and Shauna and my sister Dorothy for their ideas and encouragement. Also I would like to thank Neil Chethik for his ideas and final editing efforts and Janet Isenhour for her diligent proof reading. Also helping bring this book to its current state was Robin McBride, using her expertise in design and typesetting. Without their help this book would still be a collection of notes jotted down on everything from computer printouts to the backs of church bulletins.

Preface

Drama in the work place is like spinning tires on an icy road: There's a lot of non-productive action, some heat and noise, but very little progress. As a manager you don't need non-productive action; what you want is progress, with as little drama as possible.

Drama saps the energy and will of the people involved. Drama takes the attention of your people off what they should be doing. Drama creates bad feelings among your staff that adversely affects their ability to work together.

In the following pages, I will share with you my principles of no-drama management, a management style that I have been practicing successfully for forty years.

I worked for 25 years in management positions in a large manufacturing facility ending up as president of the company. Afterwards, I spent the next 15 years traveling between manufacturing companies acting in positions where I was responsible for all aspects of each company's success. These were turnaround situations.

These same management principles apply equally to managing a company, a department, a small group of employees, the local PTA, or any other organization in which you have been asked to provide leadership.

Why is excess drama so potentially damaging to an organization? Let's look at it in action.

Several years ago, I landed an assignment to evaluate a company that had just been put into Chapter 11. What I found was a CEO who, upon encountering any challenge, would call his staff together and explain the problem. Then he'd send his staff away to solve it. They would all rush off, dropping the last crisis they had been trying to solve, and start working on the new issue. They'd make phone calls, create spreadsheets, and investigate causes. Quickly they found themselves duplicating the same things their peers were doing. With much drama, their numerous confrontations came back to the CEO, who did little to assign specific duties. There was yelling and screaming, bad feelings, and dispirited staff. Nothing got solved. It's no wonder they were in Chapter 11.

Here's another example. Early in one of my assignments I found the company in the following situation: We had sold a lot of product and desperately needed raw materials and supplies to respond to these orders. But we had no money or credit. We did have drama, with the Sales department upset at Manufacturing for not getting the orders out fast enough and Manufacturing discouraged because of not getting materials. Purchasing blamed Finance, which pointed to Accounts Receivable as the ones at fault. It had everyone upset and complaining. It created much noise, verbal and emotional smoke, plenty of activity, but no progress toward solving the problem.

How did I deal with these dramas? How can any manager stop the noise and heat, and start making real progress? In the chapters that follow, I will show you how to encourage passion in your employees while keeping that passion focused on your goals.

———❧———

THESE BASICS OF NO-DRAMA MANAGEMENT I HAVE USED MANY TIMES. I KNOW THEY WORK.

✦1✦

Your First Day

Your first day with the new responsibility: Wow, if you're not excited and experiencing a heightened level of adrenalin, you just don't understand how much fun you're about to have. If you're nervous, that's okay too, as you might just as well start getting used to it.

Prior to starting this new assignment, ask for the name and position of each person you are likely to meet your first few days (for example: direct reports, department heads, janitors). You will then know a little about each person plus be able to call them by name. Nothing is as pleasing to the people you will be meeting as the new manager recognizing their name and having some idea of what they do. The HR department will be more than willing to provide you with this information.

I'm not kidding about the janitors. I've always made it a point to get acquainted with those people whose work assignments take them throughout the whole operation, and to treat them with respect. Not necessarily with more respect than the other employees, but certainly not with less respect. If they like your approach to management they will talk about it to everyone they come in contact with.

Someone will introduce you to your staff as the new person in charge. Say a few words about how glad you are to be there and that you will start getting acquainted very soon, then send them on their way. Do not take this time to start discussing anything major, or making vague or even specific promises. Certainly don't take this opportunity to tell them that a new sheriff is in town and how you're going to straighten them out.

Before the end of the first day call your staff together and tell them a little about your background, downplaying the successes, and explaining your management style, including your no-drama philosophy, so they know what to expect. Let them ask questions.

Set up appointments with individual staff members. Let them fit you in when they have time, and believe me they will have time. But let them know that you don't want to interfere with what they need to be doing. You want them to realize that you understand the importance of their work.

When you meet with them, spend most of your time listening and taking notes. Even if you have a certified, card carrying photographic memory, take notes. It lets the people you're talking with know you understand the importance of what they're saying and that you intend to remember it. Formally spend time with each staff member, but also spend some time casually talking with everyone you run into. These casual conversations, talking with and listening to the people you meet, can be very productive. Don't be afraid to ask what they do, even if you know. Everyone likes to talk about what they know, and as you listen you will get a good feel for how they feel about their job: excited, bored, disdainful, or proud.

Listen for a few things you can take quick action on. After all, you are probably being brought in to improve a poor situation, which means change, so find something to start that ball rolling. It may be as simple as more lighting in the lunch room, putting stripes on the parking lot, or any other small change that people would like to see happen, but haven't been able to make happen for some reason. It's important for them to see progress without any drama.

Example . . .

> In one situation there was a picket fence
> around part of the property that in the
> past someone painted white. Sections had
> now collapsed. It just gave the place a tired,
> unprofessional look.

I asked the plant manager why it was there and he told me that people wanted it taken down, but the previous president would not allow its removal. I asked him to take the fence down and clean up the area. The following day, at our first staff meeting, I asked if anyone had an attachment to the picket fence, then before they could answer told them that I was sorry if they did, but the fence was going to be gone in a few days. That was met by applause. It was a very simple thing, but it let them know there was a new manager. I didn't give them a chance to respond to my question because 1) I already knew the answer, and 2) I wanted them to know that this decision was not built on consensus, but that it was something I wanted done.

By the end of the first couple weeks you will have a good feel for what is happening and what part each staff member plays in the process, which doesn't always have much to do with their titles.

———❧———

LISTENING AND OBSERVING IS THE KEY TO FINDING OUT WHAT'S GOING ON AROUND YOU.

⇸2⇷

Let Them Help

Part of no-drama management is getting everyone engaged in improving the company. If you don't they will feel left out and that nearly always causes drama and lack of progress.

How do you do this?

Get everyone in the company looking at how to improve all operations. Start by using continuous improvement teams, which will get everyone thinking about all aspects of the operation.

To start the process, sit down with your direct reports and ask them the all encompassing question, "What can we do to lessen our costs, make us more efficient, improve our customer relations, or improve our vendor relations?" Give them some examples of breakdown questions: "Is there a better way to do this?" "What would happen if we didn't bring in this raw material today, but pushed it off until next week?" "What is the worst thing that could happen

5

if we canceled these subscriptions to *Production Weekly* or *Secretaries Digest*?" "Would the company come to a screeching halt?" "What would be the result if we didn't participate in the upcoming Industry Show?" "Could the cost of that be better spent somewhere else?" This kind of thinking should become standard operating procedure for everyone in the company. Most employees want to do a good job and want the company to succeed. They may just need to be taught how to think in terms of improved efficiency and lower expenses.

Next send them back to their own departments with instructions to meet with their people and discuss similar questions. The terms "customers" and "vendors" can also be used to mean the departments upstream and downstream from them. At a previously determined time your direct reports should come back with their ideas. Each department will primarily focus on its own operations, but that does not preclude them from bringing suggestions or questions about other departments. Sometimes people from outside a department, without a "we've always done it this way" view of things, can make some great observations. Suggestions coming in from outside a department can also cause some drama, but this is a good time for you to start training them to get results without the drama. At these sessions each direct report should be allowed, even encouraged, to bring along any of their people who can help explain an idea or answer questions.

Reviewing all the ideas should be done with all your direct reports together so they can feed off each other's excitement. These ideas, once accepted, should then be formalized, future savings calculated, calendars established, assignments given, progress tracked, improvements celebrated, and new ideas sought. This should happen on a continuous basis, no matter how well the company is doing. Many managers feel that if things are running smoothly and the company is profitable, they can stop or slow down this process. **BIG MISTAKE!** The most dangerous time for a company is when management feels they have a handle on everything and in some magical way have discovered perpetual motion. As a wise person once said, "Things get different." Situations can change quickly.

This whole process of continuous improvement can and should be exciting and fun. You'll be discussing issues that are serious and far-reaching. Your staff will not always agree, so sometimes it will become heated and loud. In another word, dramatic. It is your job to keep the drama from impeding progress or damaging relationships. This process should be something the staff looks forward to, but remember, their attitude will be a mirror image of your own.

Ask for the same input from outside people such as your sales force, the customer base, vendors, and anyone else who might be able to help. This can be done with customer or sales force focus groups or by just asking questions, orally or by questionnaire, of customers and salespeople. No one should finish speaking with a customer without asking what the company could do to help them be more profitable.

All ideas should be gotten into the hands of someone who will be attending the regular continuous improvement sessions. The customers, vendors, or anyone else who contributes an idea should get feedback, so they know they've been heard. Do this even if their ideas were not found to be something that the company could currently use.

Vendors' sales reps are another source of good ideas. These people are meeting with other businesses that are also trying to become more efficient. They see and hear about what's going on and what's working, and they usually love to talk about it. Remember these salespeople are calling on your competitors, and don't think for a minute that these competitors are not asking them what you're doing. So it's only fair that you return the favor.

Vendors are always open to discuss what you can do to help them become more efficient, therefore lowering their prices to you. Most vendors today will be very open to the idea that you are partners, and whatever either can do to make the other stronger is good for both. Your purchasing department should always be listening for new ideas about operations and new materials that are less expensive, more efficient, or of better quality.

Get as much consensus and buy-in from your management team as possible. How? Make the ideas their ideas.

Ask questions to get your continuous improvement team thinking and then listen:

> "Why do you think the efficiency in the production department is down?" You want them to come back with some original thinking including, if they are well trained, charts, graphs, numbers, or anything else to lend support to their ideas.

> "What could we do to keep this building/ office/department looking better?" You want some good ideas on keeping the workplace and common areas of the business looking more professional. Hopefully what they bring can be responded to by that well-known command "Make it so."

> "How can we reward the customer service people for the great job they did in July?" Again you're looking for ideas that will make them eager to excel again next month.

Speaking to your group of direct reports: "We've been getting some pressure to speed up our order/manufacturing/delivery cycle. Now I know this group is undoubtedly brimming with ideas on this very subject, so why don't we get back together Wednesday at 10:00 AM and go over those ideas.

The customers are telling us that if we can do this they can reach a whole new layer of customers they are trying to service." Now when Wednesday comes you need to have some ideas yourself, but listen to the others first, because if possible you want to use their ideas. Now you've done several things:

1. You've assured them that you have confidence in them.
2. You've given them an assignment to work on and a time frame.
3. You've given them the reason for the assignment and by doing that you've narrowed their focus. They might just surprise you and come back with ideas of how your customers can reach their new customers without messing with your order/manufacturing/shipping cycle. Now wouldn't that be a nice bonus!

Guide their thinking, but be subtle about it:

"If we split up the production department into two smaller departments, each with its own foreman, do you think it would improve the overall efficiency and cost per unit?" Now you've given them the germ of an idea to work on, but don't be surprised if they come back with something even better, which is what you want.

"If we put some PLEASE DON'T LIT-TER signs around the building do you think it would help keep the outside of this place looking better?" Hopefully they will come back and respond, "Yes it will, but if we put a nicely painted barrel next to each sign for the litter, and then coordinate with maintenance to see that the barrels are emptied on a regular basis, we think it will work even better." There it is, they've taken your idea and improved on it, which is just what you wanted. Your response should be something like the following: "Wow, that's great, let's do it! Now, Bill can you co-ordinate this?"

Of course the best thing you can do for this particular problem is for employees to see you picking up some of the litter yourself, on a casual basis. By casual I mean that you don't spend the afternoon policing the area, but when you see some litter, pick it up and put it in an appropriate place. Remember, lead by example.

Remember, as nice as consensus is there will be numerous situations that call for you as the manager to either say yes or no. When that time comes, be decisive. If there is no way to know which is best, then just pick one and go with it. Don't drag it out. Get the homework done and make the decision. Make sure you don't use consensus or buy-in as an excuse to procrastinate.

REMEMBER: MOTIVATE, DON'T MANIPULATE.

↠3↞

Suggest, Don't Command

Your staff will learn to know that a suggestion from you is just the way you ask them to do something. But saying "Why don't you try this," instead of saying "Go and do that," has a whole different ring to it. It makes employees feel they are part of a team. By suggesting rather than commanding, you avoid triggering anger, defensiveness, and drama. After a while your staff should be doing the same with their people, and if they aren't, explain to them the benefit of suggesting rather then commanding.

Very seldom say "I" when talking about the organization.

Say "We made this happen" Don't say "I made this happen."

Say "Why don't we try this?" Don't say "I want you to do this."

When passing out assignments, say, "Joe, why

don't you take care of this," and "Helen how about you getting us this, and I'll take care of this other thing." There should be no confusion as to who is going to do what.

One question I received from an experienced manager was "What happens if the employee doesn't take to suggestions rather than commands?" I've not experienced an employee who didn't quickly pick up on the suggestion versus the command approach, but until they do be as explicit as the situation demands. Employees who want to cooperate will catch on quickly. If they just don't want to get with the program then you might have a more serious problem.

This attitude of treating your staff as a team should become an ingrained part of your no-drama management style. Team members will feel less need to get dramatic, because they already know that their ideas and opinions are respected and will be heard.

———

THOSE WHO HAVE TO IMPLEMENT THE PLANS
SHOULD HELP MAKE THE PLANS.

⇢4⇠

First Impressions

Every company needs a continuous influx of new customers. Growth is one reason. Another reason is that old customers leave for many different reasons. Let's assume this is no reflection on the quality of product or service. So when people come into contact with your company for the first time they should come away with the best possible impression. It would be nice if we could be judged only on our products and services, but a first-time contact doesn't know about these yet. So it's up to you and your people to create an impression that keeps that prospective customer around long enough to turn them into a LOYAL customer.

Let's start with the front office receptionist and anyone else who meets the public. These people should look professional. If you are a legal firm, the receptionist should be the best-dressed person on the property. If you are an under thirty-five, engineering-for-hire firm, with all the principals wearing boots and jeans, the receptionist should still be dressed in a professional manner. If you are a fifty-person sawmill with the office in a shack, the people who meet and deal with the public should not look like they just came in from repairing the debarker.

Now, how do you get your people to dress in a professional manner without a lot of drama? One way I've seen used is to set up a comprehensive and strictly enforced dress code. I've never seen that work well, or be worth the time, effort, and drama, but if you're into self-imposed frustration and like having everyone disgusted with you, go for it.

What I have done is this, and I know it works: have an understanding with your public-meeting personnel concerning the part their appearance plays in the impression incoming people have of the company. That understanding should be part of the hiring arrangement. They need to understand what you want and why, and the important part they play in the organization. **A good way to do this is to make sure you dress professionally yourself. You know, lead by example.** And when you see one of your people dressed a little nicer than usual, thank them for looking professional. They will get the idea of the level of professional dress that you're after.

Now let's talk about the way your people act toward the public. This is so elementary as to almost be embarrassing, but every day I deal with companies that don't understand the importance of dealing with the public. The general attitude should be one of respect and wanting to be of service. The last thing you need for your people to convey is the attitude that they are superior or are being bothered by a visitor. The receptionist needs to sort out the people coming into the establishment. Not everybody knows whom they should be asking for and not everybody actually belongs there. The receptionist needs to make those determinations and give directions and help. To the person coming in the front door the receptionist needs to become their newest friend, trying to help them as much as possible. This should be done in a warm, efficient, and forthright manner. People should feel comfortable and happy. Drama in your reception area is not something you want or need.

Not everyone can combine the gatekeeping with being warm and helpful, especially at the same time. During the hiring process this should be discussed so your front office people know what is expected. Again, your example when dealing with people will go a long way in helping your employees see what you're talking about. Obviously the position of receptionist should not be the place where you start people who are being trained to do something more "important."

When you are bringing on new staff it is relatively easy to explain to them what you expect as far as how they appear and how they relate to the public and each other. But when you come into a situation where the staff has had no expectations placed on them it is a little more difficult. In this case you need to sit your staff down as a group and talk to them about the company and the part they play individually in its success. That of course includes how they appear and how they act toward the public, the company, and each other. Then explain to them your vision of how you would like outside people to view the company. By dealing with them as a group that first time you should be able to avoid the drama of any individuals feeling that you're picking on just them. If an individual can't seem to grasp the picture of what you're after, sit down with her or him and get into particulars. I've found that most people are anxious to look and act like professionals.

Example . . .

At one assignment the office manager used the receptionist position as the starting point for many of the office positions. Therefore the receptionist was always the newest and least knowledgeable person in the office. When someone came in, or called in, and asked a question, the receptionist would, more than likely, have to go and ask someone else who knew the answer. The next time that visitor made contact with the office there would more than likely be a new receptionist who was equally unknowledgeable. It gave the impression of a company that never knew what it was doing. We changed the receptionist to a fulltime, permanent position.

Example . . .

During another assignment, my office was situated so that most of the time when I left my office I walked through one end of the reception area. I made it a point to look at and nod or smile at the people waiting there, if not actually speak to them. Not that I would stop and chat, but just some kind of recognition and greeting, either verbal or nonverbal to let them know we were glad they were there.

Another idea you continually try to instill in all employees is that everyone sells. No matter what they are doing it is all part of presenting the best company face to the people you need to impress, which is everybody.

And don't forget the outside salespeople. Consider how you would react to these two salespeople coming into your office. One drives up in a beat-up old car that drips oil on your parking lot. The salesperson getting out wears frayed at the cuffs, dirty at the collar, clothes that are a virtual menu of last week's meals. This salesperson grinds out a cigar butt on your welcome mat before coming through the door and demanding of your receptionist access to you or your staff. The other salesperson gets out of a late-model clean car, dressed appropriately in clean, recently pressed attire, and when meeting your receptionist acts in a professional manner. Now, who is going to get the better hearing from you and your people? The slob may actually have the better product, but he or she may not get a fair chance to prove that.

———◦◦◦———

IF PEOPLE SEE PROFESSIONALISM, HALF
THE BATTLE TO CONVINCE THEM YOU ARE
PROFESSIONALS IS ALREADY WON.

→5←

Do It With Style

A sound management style has to be sincere and come from the heart. As trite as the heart thing may sound, it is true. A management style cannot be something you put on each morning and hope it fits, but rather what you do and who you are. Not that we can't learn or appropriate new ideas, methods, and technologies. Otherwise, no one would be reading this book. Any management style constantly evolves and hopefully gets better with each change.

A management style is always evolving. You will get new ideas and learn new techniques that make you a better manager. How do you put these new ideas and techniques into effect? It depends on what action we are talking about. If it is something like leaving your office door open instead of closed all the time, then you just start leaving it open. If it involves the way you deal with your staff or other employees then you want to change gently. Some changes you make to your style of management will be applauded by your staff. Other changes might leave your staff confused.

Example . . .

> You have been used to telling your staff each move you want them to make. Then suddenly you want them to run their departments their own way, with just some general direction from you. Your staff, not being used to that, will need some time to adjust, plus a lot of encouragement from you, and maybe even some training.

Any major change in your method of managing should be approached with a clear idea of how it will affect those around you and allowances made. For some changes an up-front, no-drama explanation, like in the above example, would certainly be appropriate. You should not be afraid of the staff seeing you change if you can honestly explain why you're changing and what you hope to accomplish by it.

If you've been using a dramatic management style and now want to move to a style that uses and tolerates less drama, your staff will need time to adjust to the change.

Leading by example seems so very basic, but many people I encounter think those they're leading should just do what they're told. People are much more apt to follow if they see you doing what you're preaching.

A management style should leave no doubt in the mind of the rest of the company that you are the leader. Being a leader means you are also the servant to everyone in the company. This may bother some, but think about what your actual job is all about:

♦ Setting direction
♦ Lending support
♦ Monitoring progress
♦ Fine-tuning direction
♦ Showing appreciation

The servant idea comes in the support area. It's your job to make sure everyone has what they need to get the job done. You've given them the job, so make sure they have the tools and resources to make it happen. This does not imply that everyone gets everything they ask for, but if you cannot explain why they cannot have additional resources, then you'd better be slow about turning down their request. If you have to turn down a request, then help them solve their problem some other way. Anytime you have to say "no" to your staff, be sure to do it in a no-drama professional manner.

—⊷⊶⊷—

YOUR JOB IS TO HELP THEM
GET THE JOB DONE.

⇥6⇤

Pass the Credit Along

Always pass credit down or up for the good things that are happening. You can't be afraid that the people you report to will not recognize your worth and the part you played in the good results. Even if you planted the idea in someone's head, give them full credit when it works out. The best thing that can happen is that people really believe it was their idea and take full ownership of the idea and the responsibility for making it work.

Don't pass credit along without a basis for giving credit. The person or people need to have been involved in the good result. It doesn't take a bloodhound to recognize when a bull's been around.

What happens if you take credit for other people's ideas? Here is one scenario: Bill works on the line and thinks he sees a good way for his department to be more efficient. After some study during his off-work hours, he approaches his boss, Charlie, who is the production manager, and explains his idea. Charlie thinks the idea has merit, but knowing it will take some additional resources, brings it to me. Now here I can go a couple ways:

I could tell the owners and staff I have a good idea, present it to them, then tell production what to do. But how will Bill feel when this idea comes back to him, garbled to some extent, but still recognizable? Bill will feel resentment and make little effort to see that the idea works.

Instead I let the rest of the staff know that a possibly good idea has come from Bill and Charlie, and that it will be studied, and if it looks feasible "it will be put in place." As part of this I make it a point to get past Bill's station and casually and professionally let him know that after looking at his idea I think it might work. Charlie, being a good manager, has already done this himself. So now Bill knows that I know the idea was his.

Then I pull together Charlie and Bill, to discuss the idea, then ask them to pull in some other people to help flesh out the idea and see the project through to completion. I want the people who came up with the idea to put it into effect. No one else in the company can match their motivation to make the idea work. Now, one more touch. When I am showing the owners around that department, I get Charlie, and Charlie, because he knows how to motivate his people, gets Bill, and I let them explain to the owners just what they are doing. This is all prefaced by my saying to the owners, "Bill came up with a great idea, and working with Charlie they . . . but let's let them explain it to you themselves."

What can this second approach do for you and your company? 1) Bill thinks you're the brightest manager around. You did like his idea. 2) He likes the feeling of being part of the team that will improve the operation. 3) He enjoys the recognition from you and the owners. 4) He will be looking for other ways to improve the operation. 5) Everyone around Bill has observed what happened with you and the owners, and the improvement that one of their own is helping to implement. They will also start trying to find ways to improve the operation.

From my experience at least 85 percent of employees want to do a good job and see the company succeed. With a little motivation this percentage can climb up to very nearly 100 percent. It just takes a little time and a personal touch on the part of you and your managers.

What do you do if Bill's idea turns out to be a flop? You just let everyone know, without any drama, that "we all thought it would work, it doesn't seem to, but that's no reason to keep from trying other ideas." Bill should get the same positive recognition, because he tried to make something better happen for the company. You desperately need to keep that attitude alive and well.

Notice when it works it's Bill's idea, and when it doesn't it's "we" who couldn't make it work. That distinction is very important.

When things go bad, don't be afraid to take the blame. If the people who report to you don't know what you're doing, you have the wrong people reporting to you. And again, if the people you report to don't understand what you're doing, than you have a bigger problem than we're talking about here.

———

AND FACE IT: IF YOU'RE IN CHARGE,
THEN YOU'RE IN CHARGE.

✦7✦

You'll Never Get All Your Coconuts Up One Tree

While talking about employees in general, a mentor once told me, "You can't get all your coconuts up one tree." What he meant was that no one individual will have all the skills and positive attributes you would like to see in any one staff member or employee. No one person will always be good at everything, always have the right attitude, always do everything the way you would do it, or always agree with you or others. No one, including you, is perfect, so get used to it. You have to decide early on if the positives in your direct reports outweigh the negatives. If they do, keep that person: if they don't, replace that person, but not before finding out if that manager is acting that way because of thinking that's the way managers are supposed to behave.

When talking to someone about their short-comings, the discussion can get dramatic in a hurry, so stay professional. If you do, your discussion will have the result of progressing toward a solution to a problem.

Example . . .

One manager put down his people because he thought they were after his job. He learned someplace that this was the way to protect his own position. I explained to him that he should be training his people instead of putting them down, and that if he didn't train someone who could replace him, I wouldn't be able to promote him. He changed his approach to management, started building his people up, instead of tearing them down, and finally got a person ready to take his place. That's when I promoted him.

Example . . .

Another manager tried to be friends with all his direct reports. They played ball (not a company team), went to the stock car races, and did many things together. He thought that was the way to treat his direct reports. It constantly kept him in hot water because these relationships got in the way of managing his people. After I explained to him that he could either be a manager or a friend, but very seldom both, he eased out of the relationships and became a good manager. In both cases, I saved a person I already knew possessed the basic skills to be a good manager.

That's just two examples of managers who were using what they felt were good management techniques, but just needed some redirection to become better. So if a staff member doesn't have all the skills you would like, try helping them improve themselves. If that doesn't work, dump them.

Your management team will not be made up of clones of yourself, thank heavens. If so, the company would be in big trouble regardless of how talented you are. The strength of the management team resides in its diversity of backgrounds, skills, and thought processes. Instead of bemoaning the fact that all your direct reports don't think like you do, revel in and take advantage of the diversity. The diversity I'm talking about doesn't encompass lack of skills or bad attitudes: it just means that everybody's skill set, the way they look at things, and the way they go about getting things done will be a little different. This is what makes for a strong team.

DIVERSITY: ACCEPT IT, ENJOY IT,
AND TAKE ADVANTAGE OF IT.

→8←

Measure It

If you don't measure it you can't manage it. This idea comes straight out of Management 101, yet many managers I've encountered feel that they have some sort of second sight or gut feel that will tell them what is going on in their organization. Only too late do they find it's only the result of their diet. If we measure our progress objectively, we end up evaluating based on facts rather than emotion; the latter is likely to result in disagreement and discord. Accurate and objective measurement is part of no-drama management.

Some managers feel that the measuring process is too expensive in time and money—but it's not nearly as expensive as not having the information. However, what if you don't have the measuring processes in place yet? Until you get them in place and develop enough historical data to feel certain of what you're seeing, you're back to basing your decisions on what your past experience tells you is right. But if you have to rely on that to any great extent, your past experience better have been extensive, and even then, one of your first priorities should be to start measuring what the company is doing.

This information collecting should, as much as possible, be integrated into your processes and systems. The more the gathering of information can be imbedded in your normal business record keeping, the less of a burden the gathering will be and the more accurate it will be.

If you don't measure, how do you know, for example, the labor and/or the material costs of what you produce? Just one area where this information becomes important is during product development.

Example . . .

> You and your group are looking at developing a *Whatsit*. The customers have asked for a *Whatsit*. Luckily, you already have some of the parts you would need for a *Whatsit*. However, pricing will be very sensitive. The group decides on the how and where of production. But without some cost information on the existing parts to give you an idea of the costs on the additional parts, you'll have to guess at whether the *Whatsit* will be profitable. If you've been measuring your costs, you have your answer.

Example . . .

By tracking incoming orders, you know how much you have to produce next week and next month. That gives you an idea on needed staffing levels and materials requirements.

You should know the activity on yesterday's incoming orders, shipments/invoicing, and cash receipts by noon today. Within a few days after the end of the accounting period, you should know how your overall labor, material, and production costs relate to product produced and sales.

Example . . .

At one assignment my CFO felt strongly about waiting until the 20th of the following month before closing the books and getting out the monthly financials. That discussion threatened to become dramatic, as I was basically questioning her assessment of what she thought could be done and when. But we cut out the drama and concentrated on what we needed and why. How? I let her help craft the solution. We compromised on getting the financials out by the 6th of the following month with 99.5 percent accuracy rather then waiting until the 20th for 100 percent accuracy. Being a professional, she soon found a way to get all her information in time to get out very accurate financials by the 6th.

Example . . .

> In one assignment, we had several
> manufacturing plants that fed numerous
> assembly/shipping plants around the United
> States. The company had grown up with
> each of these satellite plants operating on
> its own, although the home office handled
> payroll and payables. As the company
> continued to grow, it began to show all the
> indications of having excessive overhead. We
> had no individual profit and loss information
> on any of these satellite operations which
> was a problem. So before we could manage
> these branches, we needed to measure their
> performance. We developed Profit and Loss
> statements for each satellite, and then we
> sorted out the profitable ones from those
> that needed to be closed down.

Measuring has another effect. Everyone wants
to do a good job, and most people are somewhat
competitive, even if only with themselves. By
measuring, you give them a yardstick to compare
today's production with what they did last week.
With a little encouragement most employees will
try to do better than yesterday, their department
do better than last week, and their company do
better than it did last month. And it gives your
managers a natural and effective way to keep
alive and growing the competitive and continuous
improvement spirit.

Having information from actual measured performance, as compared to guesswork, will take the drama out of any discussions about how well a person, department, or the company is doing.

Department managers should keep their people up to date on how the group is measuring up. But how do you personally use this information to give encouragement and recognition? When walking through a department you mention to the people, "You put out 20 more units yesterday than you have for four months. Way to go!" Now they not only have gotten some positive recognition, but they know you're on top of things.

One important thing to keep in mind when measuring is not to let the measuring become an end unto itself. Some companies get very good at measuring their performance, but lack the skills to figure out what the information tells them. Or the problem can often be the lack of guts to do something about what is learned from the measuring. But then that's why they hired you, isn't it?

Another example . . .

At one assignment, the previous management became quite sophisticated at measuring everything, with the output very complex and voluminous. They got so enamored with measuring that they lost sight of the fact that no one used the information. Why? Because there was too much of it and they didn't understand what they were looking at; besides, no one had the time or inclination to paw through all those reports. So we sat down and established the salient indicators for each department. Then our IS department condensed all the data into what each department really needed. It amazed everyone what they could do when they got concise and non-overwhelming information.

—⟨∞⟩—

REMEMBER, IF YOU DON'T MEASURE IT, YOU CAN'T MANAGE IT.

And

KNOW THE QUESTIONS YOU ARE TRYING TO ANSWER AND MAKE SURE THE MEASURING IS RELEVANT.

→9←

Turn 'Em Loose

Part of sound no-drama management is delegating responsibility and giving your staff the authority to get the job done. Don't tell them how to do it, just give them the results you're looking for. If your staff can control what they are expected to do, they will get excited about their work but seldom find anything to be dramatic and contentious about.

How do you know if this method of no-drama management is working and your staff people are moving in the right directions and at the speed you want? Measure what they are doing as a part of the total information recording process. And occasionally ask them how the project is progressing, and how they are going about it. Ask other people questions relating to the project. Not as part of some interview, but casually. Casual questions on your part will get you a wealth of information. Wander around and keep your eyes open, and most of the time your mouth shut. However, not all information gathering on your part should be casual. A regular sit-down, how-is-it-going session with your staff and managers is indispensable.

Keep in mind that you will get numerous opinions on any one subject, so you must balance these with what you are seeing, and what the collected information tells you.

Example . . .

> At one assignment, we were having a problem getting the product moved out of finishing into shipping. We missed shipping schedules which made the customers nervous. Product backed up into the finishing department and affected efficiency. We instituted some new procedures in shipping that appeared to be having the desired effect. In my wandering around, I asked some questions of the finishing foreman. I didn't ask him how shipping was doing, but asked such things as, "Any problems getting enough product to keep the line up to capacity?" "Are the new pigments working out?" "Any problems getting the units off the end of your finishing line?" And his answer to the last question was, "Not since shipping started the new procedure." If I had asked the finishing foreman directly about how shipping was doing, that would have gotten back to the shipping foreman, and he would have

resented my asking someone besides his
supervisor about his performance. That
would have caused a dramatic confrontation.
Casual information gathering can be very
useful.

It is important for your staff, or anybody else,
to know that you won't "burn" them. By that,
I mean telling one staff person or manager what
someone else has told you about them. Burning
people will create big-time drama, absolutely no
progress, and will likely damage a relationship.
You should look for information to use in solving
problems, not for someone to blame. When your
people come to understand that, they will be open
and straightforward with you. Their next step will
be to use this same skill in dealing with the people
in their own area of responsibility, thereby making
it run smoothly and keeping their people happier.
How do you get them to do that? By letting your
people see you solving problems, not trying to find
someone to blame for each problem.

———◊◊◊———

**WHEN DEALING WITH PROBLEMS FOCUS
ON SOLUTIONS, NOT PEOPLE.**

✦10✦

Keep It Light

No matter how desperate the situation becomes, maintain a sense of humor. If you can't find anything else humorous, laugh at yourself, which will go a long way in making you appear human in the eyes of the employees. Don't take yourself too seriously, and don't let your people take themselves too seriously. Find something to laugh about in most situations. Working for, or with you, should be fun and something employees look forward to most days. Some of the harmless foibles you and your staff have may possibly become part of the corporate legend or culture.

Example . . .

At one assignment, during the inspection of the property's perimeter I went to step on the ground-level lid of an 18-inch-square concrete box that held a water turn-off valve. The lid on this box didn't fit quite right and slipped out of the way, allowing

my foot to plunge down into the valve box.
In the process of the fall, the side of my
foot hit the water valve with some force
and raised a rather neat purple bump. I
limped into the office and, as per our policy,
reported the accident and got some medical
attention.

The next day, I found a cane with a
rearview mirror attached to it leaning up
against my desk. The staff and employees
thought it hilarious. For the rest of my time
at that assignment, whenever the subject of
safety came up, I was subtly, and sometimes
not so subtly, reminded of my own problems
of watching where I was going. Several times
I brought up the incident myself when we
needed a laugh. And each time, they found
it just as amusing as the first time. Now, I
wouldn't recommend this exact action, but
what happened to me and the way I handled
it increased the morale of the employees.

Another time where humor can be of great
assistance is during moments of high drama.

Example . . .

During one Continuous Improvement
session the discussion was getting heated and
personal. The issue was about a proposed
process change. We had gone from progress
to drama. Someone made a belittling
remark about process changes in general. I

asked the group, "Would that be anything like the time I had to make an unexpected equipment change during a presentation at last year's managers meeting? The equipment in question happened to be my pants that ripped as I picked up some of my notes. This incident everyone always found funny, including me, in retrospect. The group laughed, the drama dissolved, and the meeting started to move forward again.

I recently read a book written by Peter Falk, the actor. In it, he observed that just before doing a scene he liked to find something to laugh about. It loosened him up and let his natural abilities take over. The same can be said about any work environment.

If you and your staff are having fun, you're much more apt to be productive.

———

THE KEY IS: DON'T TAKE YOURSELVES TOO SERIOUSLY, BUT TAKE WHAT YOU'RE TRYING TO ACCOMPLISH DEAD SERIOUS.

⇥11⇤

Increase Their Value

You want every employee striving to be as valuable to the company as possible. You're lucky to be in a position that allows you to build up their self-worth, their worth to the company, and their self-confidence. How?

One way is for them to watch and learn from your no-drama management style and pass it down to those they supervise including the line people. Remember: lead and teach by example.

You can also make sure that all employees have access to training programs. Such programs provide the incentive and skills to move on to more responsible positions. Everyone from your direct reports to the people on the line should have available to them knowledge on how to manage a group of people, including solving problems, resolving conflicts, and everything else that would give them the skills to move up to the next step in the organization. This training can be in the form of classes at your local community college, in-house classes, online training materials and/or classes, or off-campus seminars.

As they learn, they'll be eager to share the new knowledge, so encourage them to do so with you and with their peers. Staff meetings can be a good format for this sharing. "Judy, tell us a little of what you learned at the seminar last week." By the way, Judy should have been told she would be asked to share this new knowledge before she left for the class/seminar.

How else can you increase their value? By reinforcing, in a positive way, what they are doing right.

Give them recognition by:

Complimenting them. Make sure that the compliment is sincere and is for something truly deserved. Don't be afraid to compliment them in private or in front of their peers. You hope that your direct reports pick up on the complimenting thing and one peer compliments another.

Kidding with them. Now don't get excited and jump the rails here. Kidding may not be the right word. This may sound strange, but done right, kidding can go a long way toward making employees feel noticed, important, and part of the group. *Kidding should never tear down self-esteem or humiliate.* This of course means that you have to know the person you're kidding. Don't try it unless you know for sure that you are able to do the kidding without giving offense.

Example . . .

You're at lunch with the owners and Sharon the controller. You pay for lunch and tell the owners, "I'd better get a receipt. If I go into Sharon's office and try to collect expenses without one, I'll get thrown out." You say this in a non-dramatic way, sort of like a passing thought. You've done three good things. You've brought your controller into the forefront of the conversation and let her know that you approve of her performance. You've pointed out her tightness with the company's funds, which any owner will appreciate and increase her value in their eyes. You've done it in a way that is lighthearted and fits easily into the conversation, but still makes an important point. The owners will remember this longer than the same fact set out in a memo.

Example . . .

In a staff meeting while talking to the production vice president you say, "Al, will you be messing up our whole shipping schedule again this week by producing more than anyone expected?" In a casual way, you've complimented Al on doing a good job in front of his peers.

Another example . . .

Again at lunch with the owners and Vic,
the sales vice president, you say something
like, "Gentlemen, the problem with our
budget variances is all on account of Vic.
He and his salespeople have sold so much
product that we hired extra people and put
on another half shift to handle the volume."
Again you've done several things: brought
one of your direct reports into the limelight
in front of the owners, let them know that
he is doing an exemplary job, and that they
need to keep that in mind when they look
at the budget variances. Again it was done
in a light way that will mean more to both
the direct report and the owners then any
footnote on the financials.

Now this is my idea of kidding and might be
better called something else, but I'm sure you get
the point.

Get your people to keep up on industry news
and new ideas. And how do you do that? Read the
trade magazines yourself, then pass them along
with page markers and the initials of those you
would like to read the articles. Then, casually ask
them later what they thought of the idea, concept,
process, or whatever. They'll soon learn to keep up
with you.

—◦◦◦—

THE OBJECT IS TO SEE YOUR DIRECT
REPORTS BECOME AS SKILLED IN MANAGEMENT
AS YOU ARE. ONLY THEN CAN THE OWNERS
PROMOTE YOU AND PICK ONE OF THEM
TO DO YOUR JOB.

→12←

Increase Your Value

One of the conditions of your being able to make something of the situation you are in, or contemplating, is your ability to remain in the position and function to the fullest extent of your talents. To do that you must keep the owners happy.

Thinking like an owner will help accomplish this. Think about and answer, *If I were the owner:*

> *What would I like to see happen with my investment?*

> *What feedback would I like to get to measure the company's progress?*

> *What other communication would I like to have from my manager?*

Give the owners free access to your direct reports and anyone else in the company. Why? It is their right, and if they're diligent they'll want to do it anyway, so make it work for you. Show them you are confident in your position. Gently insist they

spend some time with your direct reports, either
formally or informally. When they are visiting and
are ready for lunch, suggest you take one or two
of your direct reports along. My experience tells
me that the more open you are the less they'll be
inclined to spend time with your people. That's just
a fact, not necessarily a reason for being open. Let
them see you are confident in yourself and your
people.

It always makes me nervous when I have
subordinates who don't want me talking to their
people. If I find out that one of them actually told
his/her people not to talk to me, I'm sure I have
someone with something to hide and I'd better find
out what that is, and soon.

Example . . .

> Early at one assignment I realized that
> the production people acted nervous around
> me. They didn't really avoid me when I
> moved around the plant, but stayed out of
> my way. This was a new experience for me
> and I thought I knew what was happening.
> Without any drama, I found out that these
> production people had been told not to
> talk to me and to leave all communication
> with me to the production manager, my
> direct report. This of course raised all
> sorts of red flags. The short version of this
> story is that the production manager was
> controlling the buying of certain key big-

ticket raw materials. In exchange he enjoyed being taken on hunting and fishing trips, using vacation lodges and other perks he enjoyed from these suppliers. After changing production managers and having a serious talk with the purchasing manager, I found that people became more than happy to be seen talking with me.

Trust the owners, when talking to your people, to know the questions to ask and how to interpret the answers. If the owners are fully "in the picture" they will be a lot less likely to say or do the wrong thing when dealing with your people.

Another way to increase your value will be to learn what you can about new ideas and products, and let the owners know what you've learned. Not in some formal memo, but by dropping a no-drama comment on them such as, "I saw in a recent trade magazine an article that the new computerized milling machines will do such and such. We will need that technology someday, but we're not ready for it yet." Or, "At the Trade Show, I sat in on a seminar about inventory control and picked up an idea about controlling small tools that we are going to try." This will give the owners the idea that you're 1) looking for ways to improve their operations, 2) open to new ways to improve their operations, and 3) using what you've found to improve their operations. They'll love it.

Every manager will experience situations in which he or she must take specific actions, in order to get specific results. Keep track of your SARS (Situations, Actions, and Results). Again let the owners subtly know what you've accomplished. Most of the time these things will have been a group endeavor and you will explain them that way: "We've done this, we've made this happen, we got this to work." However you're the one in charge and the owners will understand that you are the one managing the company.

These SARS will also come in handy if you need to sell yourself to other owners in the future.

———✺———

YOU WANT THE OWNERS TO SEE YOU
AS MORE VALUABLE TO THEM TODAY
THAN YOU WERE YESTERDAY.

→13←

Don't Try to Make Chicken Soup Out of Chicken Manure

One problem that most even slightly compassionate managers have when dealing with people is in trying to make something out of the wrong ingredients.

Example . . .

People—I once inherited a manager who always said the right thing in the wrong way to his people. He could hardly say "good morning" without irritating them. I knew he could do it right because he did it right with me and with his peers. We discussed the reason for the response he got from his departments. He knew there was a problem and would promise to correct it, but never really could. Soon I realized that the root of his problem revolved around his basic lack of respect for the people who were working for him. After talking with him about this aspect of his behavior, I came to realize that he wasn't going to change and I let him go. I could have fooled around and tried to make something out of the situation, but he just wasn't worth the continual turmoil and drama his mouth caused. Technically he was great, but the company was better off without him.

The same problem is prevalent in non-personnel areas as well.

Example . . .

Product—After getting input from our customer base, we developed a product line that we felt would do great things. The customers felt good about it, we felt good about it, and the sales force felt good about it. We introduced the new line at a national trade show and got great reviews. The only problem, no one placed any orders. We reviewed the situation and couldn't come up with any reasons why it shouldn't sell. But it didn't, so instead of fiddling around and trying to make something out of what looked to be nothing, we bagged the project and went on to something else.

Another example . . .

At one assignment, the owners asked me to investigate a company they had their eye on. They were looking for help in reaching a purchasing decision. It was in the same industry, so would have fit nicely into the several companies they already owned. I spent some time at this other company watching the operation and analyzing its records. What I found was a lot of activity and high drama, people rushing around mostly out of breath, a crisis around every corner, and multiple people working on every problem. The product was okay, but in a category with not much room for growth. When I put all this together I told the owners they should pass on this deal, which they did. Most of the problems I saw could have been ironed out, given time, and would have been fun to work on, but the owners and I didn't need all that right then.

In these situations, you as the manager have to be able to determine if you have a viable situation, or if you have chicken manure. Experience can be a big help. But what if you haven't developed that much experience? You get as much input from those around you as you can in a reasonable time, then make the decision. That can be rather lonely, but that's why they hired you, right?

—◦◊◦—

IF YOU HAVE CONCLUDED THAT
THE SITUATION IS NOT GOING TO
WORK, MAKE THE CHANGES NECESSARY
AND GET ON WITH LIFE.

→14←

Be a Role Model

Part of your job is to teach and train those around you. Everything you do and say should be done with that in mind.

Dress like you want your people to dress. If you are trying to raise the standard of dress in the front office for example, occasionally compliment the people who are dressed professionally. Be careful of how you word these compliments. You're trying to make them glad for dressing as they did, not make them feel uncomfortable.

Talk like you want your people to talk. If you don't want your people using four-letter words, then never use them yourself. If you don't use them, they won't, at least not in front of you, and they will use them less when away from you.

If you don't want your direct reports to let drama get in the way of progress in their departments, then don't let drama get in the way of progress when dealing with your staff.

Demonstrate the work ethic you want your people to have. Some of your work is going to be invisible to your direct reports, so how do you let them know that you worked half the night on something for the company? First of all you let them know in a very subtle way, working it into the conversation while downplaying your efforts. Like saying, "Maybe if I'd known more about this software it wouldn't have taken me until three this morning to get this done." They will notice the time you come to work and the time you leave. Be as prompt as you want them to be.

Example . . .

When at lunch with several of your people make it a point to get them back on time, just as you would want them to do if you weren't there.

Example . . .

If you're going to be late in the morning, inform the person who is going to be asked "Where's the boss?" And let them know why you're away, unless it's extremely personal. Like: "I'll be attending a Chamber Board breakfast in the morning, but I should be in by 10, and if not, I'll call." You want to know where your people are during the workday, and they have a right to know how to reach you and when to expect you.

Show energy in your speech, in your actions, in your decision-making.

Example . . .

> When you're in a meeting, don't always just sit there, occasionally get up and walk around when you're talking, but stand still when you're listening. I'm not talking about acting nervous or twitchy, but projecting the fact that you're so excited about what is going on you can't sit still. You're the leader, so if you're not energized by what the company's doing, chances are nobody else will be.

If you don't want your managers treating the line workers like second class citizens, then you must always treat those employees with respect—in person and when talking with others. Show them respect with the policies you develop and with the changes that are made. Show them respect in the information you share with them. Show them respect by being truthful with them, and show them respect by including them in the decisions that affect them. If you show the employees respect, your managers will show them respect, but if they don't, insist they do. The importance of treating all employees with respect should be self-evident, but let's talk about it a little more anyway. Besides just following the golden rule, these people are the ones making the product, repairing the machinery, keeping the restrooms clean, selling the product, servicing the customers, writing the programs, doing the office work, and generating the income that drives the company. And for that, if for no other reason, they deserve the respect of everyone. I always thought of it this way: If the janitor and I each took a week off, whose absence would be noticed first and most? Very probably the janitor.

In your conversations and in your memos and letters, don't forget to say "please" and "thank you." It's not painful, and the little bit of time it takes will pay dividends. Not necessarily big dividends but any dividend is a plus. And don't forget, you're trying to teach your people how to manage, and courtesy is an important part of good management. Good manners will often sidetrack drama.

You want your people working together. Everyone has their assigned responsibilities, but if someone needs help you want surrounding people to jump in.

Example . . .

When you're walking through the plant and you come up to a place where the forklift driver has spilled a load, stop and help him pick it up. Why? Because you want people to see this helpful spirit in action.

Example . . .

If you see a new person trying to figure out how to load paper in the copy machine and obviously not sure what they're doing, stop and give them a hand while teaching them how to do it.

Example . . .

When walking through the plant and meeting a forklift at an intersection I always stop and motion the forklift to proceed first. Why? Because I want the forklift driver and anyone else who is watching to understand that what the driver is doing at the moment is more important than what I'm doing or at the very least as important.

Another example . . .

I would do the same thing when sitting and discussing something with the Controller. If one of the Controller's direct reports came in out of breath with some emergency I let them go ahead and get an answer from their supervisor before continuing on with my own discussion. As I said, it's a small thing, but the small things can make a difference. If I had something to discuss with the Controller, and I didn't want any interruptions, I closed the door.

———❧———

BE A ROLE MODEL BY SHOWING YOUR EMPLOYEES HOW TO FOLLOW THE COMPANY'S RULES, REGULATIONS, AND POLICIES.

→15←

Cutting Out and Replacing the Dead Wood

At some point, you will have to terminate staff members. By the time it's necessary to fire people, they should be expecting it to happen. Why? Because you've been honest about their inadequacies. In fact, if you do it right, inadequate employees will usually quit because they realize their talents and your needs do not match. If it does come down to firing one of your staff, do several things:

Make it short and to the point. Remember, no drama.

Do not solicit a response.

Make your statement in such a way that there is no question about the outcome. Again, no drama.

Be compassionate. If this is hard for you to do, imagine being on the other side of your desk.

This is not the time or the place for self-gratification. By self-gratification I mean this: You might think this a good time to really tell your staff person what you think, how you feel, what others think, or the pain they have been in the posterior of the company and you. This is not the time or the place for you to vent those feelings. Again no drama, just straight-forward professionalism.

Have someone with you when you're firing this employee, preferably your Human Resources person. In the first place you need a witness to the proceedings, someone keeping notes on what you do and say. In the second place, it will give your Human Resources person another look at how a firing should be handled, and the fact that they see you doing it in an efficient, compassionate, and sensitive way will not hurt your standing with the staff.

When you're firing someone, you should experience three emotions:

♦ Glad to see them go because they are not good for the company.
♦ Empathy.
♦ A letdown because of your inability to coach this person into becoming what the company needed or inability to find a slot where this person could meet the company's expectations.

When it comes time to replace the person you just fired, the best possible place to look can be within your own organization. Why? These are people you already know and have worked with and who know you. That's important because they know what they are getting into by accepting more responsibilities.

Example . . .

At one assignment I had to replace a plant manager. Whom did I pick to replace that person? My purchasing manager. She didn't have all the technical knowledge of her predecessor, but I knew that she knew how to recognize and use the people who did have the technical expertise. Most important, I knew that she knew what she didn't know and wasn't afraid to ask questions and learn. She got along well with the people above, below, and at her level of the organization, and she was well respected. Some people thought I was crazy, but it worked out even better then I expected.

But let's say you have no one in the organization you can promote so you have to look outside. Remember the person you interview may not be quite the person you hire. Let me put it another way. A fairly intelligent interviewee, who can read all the advice on interviewing, can figure out how to handle most any question you ask. So I always like to ask some questions in a traditional interview format, then get them into the work environment, meet some people, and talk about what they see going on. Find out how this environment relates to where they have been, or what they have studied, and see how they react. Do they get excited when they see the work environment, do they ask good questions? Do they relate well to the people they meet, either the ones they will be reporting to or the ones that may be reporting to them, and especially with the later, do they relate to them with respect? Remember, you are looking for someone who not only has the skills, but also has ideas and opinions, not necessarily just like yours. You already have you, what you want is someone who can bring in additional ideas and opinions.

Explain your no-drama management style and see how they react.

—◆◆◆—

TRY TO MAKE SURE THAT THE NEW PEOPLE YOU BRING IN ARE WILLING TO LEARN AND CHANGE.

✦16✦

Building the Team

To help build your team, you need your people not only trusting you, but trusting each other. They have to feel comfortable that their peers will do their jobs and do them right, just as they will do their own jobs and do them right. How can you build that team trust?

Keeping your office door open at all times will help build this trust. This sounds so simple, but think about it. You're in your office and someone comes to talk. You close the door. The next person comes along and seeing the door closed thinks, "Who's in with the boss, and why the closed door? Why am I not in there with them?" Or they might think: "Are they talking about me?" Multiply this scenario by the times there could be someone in your office behind closed doors and you can see what can gradually build up in the minds of your direct reports.

The only time to disregard this open-door policy is when the subject matter happens to be so personally or corporately sensitive that you can't risk letting anyone overhear. In a clean-running operation, this should seldom happen.

Never make it evident that one direct report and you have been talking about the personal effectiveness of a third direct report or their department. If a direct report wants to talk to you about one of his or her peers, the best thing you can do is listen. This can get very dramatic, and it's up to you to keep the drama from driving the situation. The worst thing you can do is openly agree with the person. If some action seems appropriate concerning this third party, tell the complainer that you'll work on it. Nothing more. Don't say what you'll do, or that you'll get back to them. If they trust you they'll be satisfied with that. Of course if a problem exists you've got to handle it.

Don't burn people.

Example . . .

> At one assignment, the sales manager came steaming into my office. She informed me that shipping recently not only shipped an order late, but wrong, and then had been rude to the customer when he inquired about the whole mess. She finished up by saying, "If something isn't done about shipping, we won't have any customers at all." Then she sat there looking expectantly at me. My no-drama response to her was,

"Thanks for the information." That left me with several choices.

I could have burned the sales manager by going to the operations manager and telling him that the sales manager said such and such. His response to that would have been dramatic, including some excuses and a couple reasons about how it must have been the fault of sales all along. Following that, both sales and operations would take every opportunity to bad-mouth each other. In which case I would have burned the sales manager and taken the whole thing up to another dramatic level, away from a no-drama management style.

Instead, I asked the operations manager how we were doing on getting deliveries out on time. If he had said we were doing okay, I would have pressed him for more specific information on that particular customer. In this case the operations manager already knew about the incident. He was more than happy to explain what he had done about it and to state it would not be happening again. Except for the original incident, he felt good about what he had done, I felt good about what had been done, and I suggested that he sit down with the sales manager and bring her up to speed on the situation, which he was glad to do.

If you have to have employees mad at

someone, it is better to have them mad at
you rather than at each other. Please read
that last sentence again. You need the people
who are working together every day feeling
as good about each other as possible.

Example . . .

On one of my assignments, I found myself
in a situation where the previous CEO had
forbidden the office people from talking
with any of the manufacturing people. He
was the go-between person, and with very
little problem kept both factions mad and
upset with each other. He felt that he could
better control both entities by doing so.

When I got there, I made it plain that
I did not intend to be in the go-between
business, and that they should be dealing
directly with each other. Manufacturing
was welcome in the office, and the office
was welcome in manufacturing. This new
strained working relationship took time
to smooth out, but soon the office and
manufacturing came to see that they both
wanted the same thing and discovered
that they could work together. My part in
this process was only a little nudging and
encouragement. The overall effect was a
much stronger team of managers.

If you want your team to function at top
proficiency you will not put up fences between the

team members. By fences, I mean reasons for team members to dislike, distrust, or feel superior to one another. It is easy for a manager to put up fences. It is much harder to take them down and keep them down. Your team members all have different personalities, different levels of people skills, different degrees of passion for their work, and different skill levels in their own areas. That alone can cause lots of drama. So how do you keep them from disliking, distrusting, or feeling superior to those around them? How do you alleviate the drama? You have to get employees to see each other as individuals who can contribute by using their skills and passion for the company goals. And how do you do that? You do that by showing them that you see them as contributing individuals, each with value, and by gently letting them know that no one has 100 percent of all the knowledge, attributes, or skills—not even yourself.

You can gain a great deal of information by just listening and keeping your mouth shut. Many managers feel they're not being managerial unless they're talking. But face it, when you're talking you're not learning anything you don't already know.

—⟶∘∿∘⟵—

By LISTENING, YOU CAN LEARN A LOT.
REMEMBER THE ADAGE, "MOST PEOPLE
DON'T LISTEN, THEY JUST WAIT TO TALK."
DON'T BE ONE OF THEM!

→17←

Be Cool

Never get angry at people or situations, or at the very least, never act like you're angry. The type of anger I'm talking about is on-the-edge-of-being-out-of-control anger. You don't want to train your people to wait until they see you get red in the face and about ready to "blow" before they think they have to react to what you're trying to get done. Occasionally, anger, if used surgically, can be useful. But this should be a shocking occurrence to your people, mostly because they see it so very seldom.

Anger leads to high drama which should not be part of your management style. In meetings, it will be easy for people who feel passionately about what they're doing to get angry with their co-workers and resort to dramatic speech and actions. This passion, not the anger, is something you want, and some heated discussion should be normal and healthy. If that heated discussion starts to get personal or moves to the point where it's not accomplishing positive progress, you need to redirect the energy away from being wasted on drama.

Example . . .

At one assignment the maintenance manager asked me to go out and look at a broken water main on the back side of the plant. It was very cold outside so part of the small pond this leak had created was frozen. The manager warned me that this pond was liquid on top, but frozen underneath and slick. Nonetheless, I launched myself across one finger of this pond, successfully landing on the far side, where my feet went out from under me and I sat down in the icy water. I could have been humiliated, and angry, but instead I laughed and carried on with the inspection of the problem. During the days following I kept getting comments like "Didn't we tell you that was a private pool?" "Was the water cold enough for you? "If you'd let us know, we would have brought a snorkel and some flippers." They really seemed to like that one as I heard it in just about every department during the next few days. The camaraderie fostered by my staying cool (no pun intended) gave the company another little nudge toward success. Now if I had gotten angry and dramatically blown my stack, the employees would have been embarrassed for me and would have whispered about this incident behind my back. That would not have been good for the morale of the company.

Example . . .

At another assignment, I was partially lying under a piece of malfunctioning equipment looking at the problem being explained to me. An employee, trying to help, made an adjustment that dropped several large blobs of grease on my white dress shirt. The employee turned pale, expecting the worst. The conversation about the machine came to a sudden halt as everybody held their breath. I ignored the grease and continued with my questions about the problem. After getting up, I smiled at the employee, who handed me a rag, and as I wiped the grease off my shirt, not very successfully, said, "I was getting sort of creaky anyway." The story of that incident went through the plant in record time, and ever after, I was known as a "cool" guy. That helped me later in my ability to be a successful no-drama manager. To be a successful manager, you don't need the love of your people, but you do need their respect. Staying "cool" can be one way to earn that respect. In this particular situation, I accomplished three things:

♦ People saw that I didn't get angry with employees when they made honest mistakes.

♦ They saw that I wasn't afraid to get dirty in the pursuit of getting that machine back into operation.

♦ They saw that I was able to laugh at myself, so later on when I kidded them, they knew I was laughing with them and not at them.

Both of these situations made for more respect, which increased my ability to manage.

—◦◦◦—

STAYING COOL IN THE FACE OF SITUATIONS THAT COULD OR USUALLY WOULD PRODUCE ANGER AND DRAMA CAN RESULT IN REAL AND SUBSTANTIAL DIVIDENDS.

→18←

Leave Them Smiling

Occasionally, you will have a direct report who has messed up. As soon as possible after you've decided that person needs to be talked to, do it. Don't drag it out. If you wait too long, he or she will think you don't care. If you move too soon, you stand a good chance of overreacting, or working from a wrong conclusion. Very seldom do you run into a situation that needs immediate action, but occasionally it happens. This situation should be approached professionally and with as little drama as possible.

So now the person has messed up and the time has come to talk. This is not a termination-type situation, so say without any drama, "Joe, what happened?" And then listen. This can be a good time to get a better insight into what makes Joe tick. Will he be straightforward about accepting responsibility for the mess? What you hear during this conversation will tell you a lot about his management style and management maturity. After all, one reason for this session should be to help him be a better manager.

Let him tell you what he has learned and how he would handle the same situation again.

Once you've completed the "don't do it again" talk, raise a positive topic before the person exits your office. Devote extra attention to this topic. You want the employee to feel upbeat and energized when he or she returns to work.

People will know the reason for Joe's visit to your office and will be waiting to check his attitude when he leaves. Seeing him leaving in an upbeat mood will do a lot for the other people in the organization. It will cut down on the fear factor, and that is one of the things you're after. You want people to realize it's not good to mess up and that they will get a chance to explain and discuss the situation without getting their heads handed to them.

The effect on Joe?

- ♦ He knows he messed up.
- ♦ He knows he has been "talked" to without any drama.
- ♦ He now realizes that messing up is not fatal.
- ♦ He now realizes that taking the blame is the mature thing to do.

♦ He feels good about the session, as he has left with something positive on his mind.

♦ His attitude will be passed on to the other people in the company.

The personal benefits are that when you mess up, and you will, and take credit for it, as you should, people will not make a big dramatic deal of it, just as you don't make a big dramatic deal of it with them.

Example . . .

A departmental manager blew his cool when talking to one of his people about messing up and ruining some product. Soon, the situation became well known all over the plant. I pulled him in, and after listening to his explanation (in this instance he admitted he had screwed up), asked him if he thought his dramatic outburst had enhanced his ability to manage?" He admitted that it hadn't. Knowing Tom could draw all the right conclusions, I moved on to how we could recover from the production problem. He was proud of the fact that he, along with the person who ruined the product, came up with a plan of recovery and put it in motion. I let him explain this plan in detail, just to give him something positive to talk about, then complimented him on the quick action and sent him on his way.

Example . . .

Our accounts payable person had inadvertently paid the wrong vendor for a shipment of materials. The check would possibly be hard to recover. It was a serious situation as there was considerable money involved. The controller had brought the accounts payable person into my office for an additional talking to. Everyone in the office saw her being brought into my office and knew why. This person was a good employee and even though we all wanted to get our money back, we also wanted to salvage the employee. We discussed what she had done, why it happened, how we could recover our money, and what we could do in the future to prevent it from happening again.

When we were through, I brought up the anecdote about her husband, a department foreman, who recently found a stray dog wandering in his area with some very humorous results. We were still smiling about this when she and the controller left my office.

———

IF AT ALL POSSIBLE, LEAVE PEOPLE IN A
POSITIVE MOOD BY THE TIME THEY'RE
THROUGH INTERACTING WITH YOU.

→19←

The Fear Factor

It is impossible for you or your people to practice or learn sound no-drama management while being afraid of making mistakes.

Let's expand on this fear factor. You need all your people in a frame of mind that allows them to act, make decisions, or initiate programs, without a paralyzing fear of failure. They must be concerned with failure, but not to the point that it keeps them from doing their job effectively.

How do you accomplish this?

By not being dramatic when someone makes a mistake. Don't dwell on the mistake maker, but on how to fix the mistake. Let them know that if they do make a mistake, it does not make them a bad or incompetent person. Only people who aren't doing anything will be free of mistakes. And that's a mistake. The more they do, the more mistakes they will make along the way, and don't forget, the more they will learn. Remember this applies to everyone, including you. Someone once said, "Good judgment comes from experience, and a lotta that comes from bad judgment." All members of your management team should get to the point where they can, without drama, readily admit making a mistake. Then a solution can be found rather then castigating the mistake maker, which will be a waste of time and counterproductive. Or better yet, when they report the mistake they will have already worked out a solution.

One way your people will learn how to own up to mistakes will be by watching you. When they see you make a mistake, they should also see you take responsibility for that mistake and have a plan ready for correcting the mistake. Then they will know how to handle their own mistakes.

If you do have a person who seems to make more mistakes than what their accomplishments would deem necessary, then you may have them in the wrong place, trying to do something they're not suited to do.

There are other kinds of fear than just from making mistakes.

Example . . .

> At one assignment I inherited a department manager who tried to make a friend out of each of her staff members. She felt they needed to love her and feared they didn't. If she thought her staff members

were forming friendships within their own
ranks, she played them against each other
to stifle those budding friendships. Her
emotions ran the gamut of *do-whatever-
you-like*, to *don't-pick-up-that-pencil-without-
instructions*. Her people never knew what to
expect from her and therefore worked in a
state of continual fear. People did not respect
her and transferred out of her department
as soon as possible. Turmoil and drama
continually surrounded her. Even though she
was technically competent and bright, the
company could not afford her and the drama
she created.

Example . . .

At another assignment the previous
president had played each department off
against each other in order to maintain some
kind of control over the company and its
people. By the way, this never really works
except to keep up a continuous state of
high drama and lack of progress. When I
entered the picture, each department was
afraid to interact with the people in any
other department. They lacked cohesive
team spirit or a spirit of cooperation. One
of my first actions was to not talk about
department #1 to department #2 without
department #1 being present. They soon
got the idea that what they saw and heard
was exactly what they got, without any

hidden agendas or drama. And it amazed
them how quickly the fear dropped away,
and they were all interacting as a no-drama
management team.

—————

EmplOYEES HAVE THE RIGHT TO KNOW
WHAT EMOTIONAL RESPONSE TO EXPECT
FROM YOU IN NEARLY EVERY SITUATION
THAT MIGHT COME UP.

⇝20⇜

Thou Shalt Not Lie

Never lie to your people. This is No-Drama Management 101. Your people need to know that when you tell them something, they can bank on it. If you tell them you're going to do something, do it. If circumstances change and you can't do it, let them know as soon as possible. Treat them like you expect them to treat you. If you don't, they won't, because you're setting the tone. So what do you do when you are asked a question you just can't answer because of its sensitivity or some other valid reason? Simply, without drama, tell the person, "Sorry, but I can't discuss that with you at this time, but when I can, I will." That sounds simple, but it's not always that easy to put into practice. If you haven't lied to them before, they will believe you.

If your staff and other employees have to spend time deciding if you are being honest with them, your chance of being a successful manager will be in doubt.

Example . . .

At one assignment, I found the situation so desperate that it became plain we should either lay people off or institute a wage cut. But the order file was full and we needed everyone. During a general meeting of all the employees, after explaining in some detail the company's financial situation, I announced, without any drama, a wage cut. I also explained the plan of how they would recover their lost wages, and what would need to take place for that to happen. It would depend on the company meeting some specific performance goals.

Then came the big question. "Mr. Spady, do you really think the company can reach that level of performance again?" I could have given them a bunch of verbiage and probably made them feel good, but not necessarily any more informed. I just told them that I hoped it would, and thought it would, but could not really assure them that it would absolutely happen. An aside: It helped this whole situation when the employees found out I was taking a larger percentage cut than anyone else. Thanks to the efforts of everyone, the company reached its goals and the people recouped their lost wages.

Example . . .

At another assignment, we had turned the company around enough that it became attractive to a possible buyer. This buyer made an offer to our owners and as part of the process brought in a team to start the due diligence. The employees knew something was going on, and they finally came right out and asked. The owners weren't excited about the news of a possible sale becoming common knowledge, but I felt that after all the hard work this group put forth to turn the company around, they deserved the truth, and the owners finally agreed. The employees rewarded our trust by doing an admirable job of keeping the possible sale confidential. Being honest with the employees about what might happen eliminated most of the drama when it did happen.

———⟋⟋⟋———

THERE IS NO QUICKER WAY TO LET THE STAFF AND OTHER EMPLOYEES KNOW THEY ARE PART OF THE TEAM THAN BY TELLING THEM THE TRUTH!

→21←

Chain of Command

Never circumvent the chain of command. This is a basic of no-drama management. If people complain to you about their supervisor, the first question you ask them should be, "Have you talked to your supervisor about this?" If they answer in the negative, tell them that should be the first thing they need to do. If their supervisor happens to be one of your direct reports, tell them if they are not satisfied after the talk with their boss, they can come back to you. If the complaint is of a personal nature, (such as sexual harassment), send them to the personnel director. If the complaint is a for-your-information type of thing, then just tuck it away among those little gray cells and compare it to other things you are hearing or seeing. Maintain confidentiality when someone comes to you with a complaint or information about a problem, even if that action seems to be ill-intentioned. In a well-managed environment, where the supervisors and your direct reports have been trained to listen, very few complaints will reach you.

If you see something going on that you question (unless it's life threatening or a major safety hazard), go to the direct report who has the responsibility for that area and let that person handle it. Again, don't tell your people what to do, just what you saw; they'll figure out a solution. The next time you're in that area, watch to see if the behavior or condition has been corrected.

Example . . .

> While walking through the plant, I came through a door and found a forklift driver sitting on his machine smoking a cigarette. This happened in a woodworking plant, with dry wood dust, dry wood chips, dry sawdust, and dry lumber all around. Do you get the idea that the environment was rather flammable? From that position, both the driver and I could see several "NO SMOKING" signs. Without any drama, I asked him to put out the cigarette, took the key out of his forklift, and asked him to report to his supervisor. I then took the key and gave it to the production manager (my direct report), told him what happened, and that the employee was on his way to see his supervisor. I trusted the supervisor and the production manager to do the right thing, and they did.

Example . . .

One day as I walked through the sawmill, I spotted an employee trying to dislodge a slab of wood that was stuck and plugging up the conveyor into the chipper. Now this conveyor ran a little below floor level, with safety railings along both sides, but this employee felt compelled to climb over the railing so that he could personally attack the misbehaving slab of stuck wood. Because slabs occasionally got jammed up, we placed wood poles along the conveyor to use in dislodging them. This genius was trying to do it while balancing on one foot and kicking at the slab with the other foot. I walked up to him, grabbed him by a flailing arm, and pulled him back from the conveyor. I hung on to him until he got back over the rail, then explained to him that his action constituted a gross safety violation and that he should be using one of the wood poles. I also told him that he would hear from his supervisor, which he did.

These were two cases where I felt the message couldn't wait to go through the chain of command. But the times during my career that I've felt I needed to do this can be counted on one hand.

Again, a basic premise of no-drama management: Don't go to your direct report's employees and tell them what to do. And why should you?

That's what you're paying your direct report to do. Ignoring the chain of command usually leads to drama, the clouding of areas of responsibilities, and the lack of progress.

Two more thoughts on this: If you have enough free time to be managing your direct report's area, something is wrong. If you feel you need to manage a direct report's area, then get the direct report out of the way and do the job yourself. Every employee should get instructions from only one supervisor. Otherwise a lot of drama and lost progress will result.

You should always be looking for someone to compliment, but be very careful how you compliment people who report to someone else. You might see an employee who looks like they're working hard and doing things right, but they might not be doing what their supervisor asked them to do. In that case, your compliment creates a dramatic problem for this supervisor.

So how do you deal with people who don't report to you? Smile a lot, make eye contact, nod, wave, ask them "how's it going?" or "how're you doing?" Don't use these last two unless they are in a position to talk. Use the person's name if you know it. This can be done casually, but personably. Look the person in the eye, so they know you're seeing them and not just another one of the employees. If a conversation results, you have a great opportunity to ask a few questions and get a feel for how these employees feel things are going in their area. Again, you tuck this information away and see how it compares with other things you see and hear.

This doesn't preclude your making a complimentary remark to an employee who according to the supervisor has been doing a good job. You can say, "I've heard good things about what you're doing." This not only builds up the worker, but his supervisor as well, because that person then knows his supervisor has been talking to you about him in a positive way. Ergo, the supervisor must be very smart.

—◈◈◈—

PART OF YOUR JOB IS TO LET THEM DO THEIR JOBS.

→22←

Involvement Is the Key

For the company to succeed, everyone must be innovative and imaginative. To make this happen, you'll need not only your but everyone else's ideas on how to improve. The old "THINK OUTSIDE THE BOX" cliché has been beaten to death, but always comes back. Why? Because it's good advice! However, it's not always easy to do. The tendency is to think in terms of what's being done, or has been done, or tried, or talked about before.

Sometimes, too much historical knowledge can almost be a detriment to thinking outside the box. We tend to look at what is or has been, instead of what can be. Success is another thing that may slow down innovation. That sounds silly, as innovation has probably played a big part in making the company a success, but many times people are afraid to mess with success. Remember, things get different. Today's successful idea, or process, might not work or be the best solution tomorrow, and everyone needs to be thinking of innovations. To remain successful, everyone will have to work at making changes that will further improve the company.

Part of no-drama management will be to overcome the tendency to stick to the tried and maybe or maybe not true. Never throw out any idea just because it sounds strange, goofy, crazy, or new. The process of inspecting, accepting, and rejecting new ideas can be filled with drama. It's up to you to exert your no-drama style and maintain positive progress.

Sometimes new people are ignored, because the old-timers think they will not understand the fine points of the problem. However, these new people will not be aware of what has been tried before, or what the general consensus says won't work. In other words, they can look on the problem with a fresh set of eyes, and their input should not be discouraged.

Example . . .

> A group of us were standing and watching the flow of product from one machine center to another machine center. That particular machine configuration dated back many years. But the machining needs had recently changed, and we needed to figure out how to get materials from one machine, cutting out one process, over

to another machine. While this group of geniuses deliberated over the situation, Bill, a relatively new employee and one of the machine operators, came by. Thinking that if these managers could stand around scratching their heads, he might as well do the same, he stopped beside me to look over the situation. I explained to him what we were trying to do. He responded, "Why don't you just move the machine over here?" Now Bill was so new he didn't realize this process had worked for many years, so saw nothing wrong with his suggestion. And there was nothing wrong with his idea, so we did exactly what he suggested: We moved the machine to the work. And we made sure that Bill got the credit.

Example . . .

At all my assignments, we tried to make the vendor reps feel like part of our family. At one company, we developed a production bottleneck that we, as brilliant as we were, just couldn't figure out. So we took three vendor reps whose products impacted on that particular process, showed them what we wanted to do, and asked for their help in solving the problem. Within a week, all three came back with several ideas, most of them good. We picked one idea and put it into effect. We took all three reps out to a nice lunch to thank them for their efforts and to

make them feel even more like they were
part of our family.

———◈———

PEOPLE SHOULD BE APPLAUDED FOR BRINGING UP IDEAS, WHETHER THEY'RE GOOD IDEAS OR NOT.

→23←

Share the Information

Give all the information you can to the people making the decisions in your operation. Remember, most information is accumulated so your managers can manage better. It may be that you will have to help them understand the information, but that's part of management. This doesn't mean full financial disclosure to everyone in the organization, but certainly the disclosure of information pertaining to any manager's area of responsibility. And this absolutely should contain the information they are helping collect. They need to know and be able to explain to their people why measuring is important.

Good information will reduce the drama during discussions of what should and shouldn't be done to improve the operations.

Example . . .

> At one assignment, we operated branch
> factories all over the U.S. The company

desperately looked for ways to cut costs. The problem was we didn't have separate profit-and-loss information on these operations. After we developed cost figures for each plant, managers found it possible to help us ascertain what needed to be done to get their plants profitable. The result was that we cut expenses and improved profits. And the most important and more far-reaching result, the managers felt like managers and not just babysitters.

Example . . .

At another assignment, in order to make my direct reports more effective, I trained them to read the financials. Once they could do that, they were able to equate the decisions they were making in their departments to how it would affect those financials. These people soon started to see efficiency possibilities we might have otherwise overlooked, or just ignored, without detailed information. And just like the plant managers in the previous example, they started feeling like real managers. And guess what? They thrived on it!

———

REMEMBER, THE MORE THEY KNOW,
THE BETTER THEY CAN MANAGE.

→24←

Don't Accept Monkeys

One time, I watched an organ grinder plying his trade on a busy street. Watching what happened reminded me of something I had seen in a video seminar years before. He had a monkey on a leash, collecting donations in a tin cup. Whenever the monkey became frightened or disturbed, it would jump onto the shoulders of the organ grinder, and it was with difficulty that the music man got the monkey to let go and get back to work.

It can be the same for you as a manager when your people find a problem and their first inclination is to bring it to you to solve.

Don't let your people bring you problems, drop them on your back like a pet monkey, and then walk away. When your people do bring you problems, they should know they must also bring along solutions. When you first institute this procedure it might get a dramatic response, but your no-drama style will handle that.

Train your staff not to attach problems to you for solving. Ask them to go back and generate some solutions and bring them back to you. Explain to them that since they are so close to the problem, you're sure they are the best ones to come up with solutions. You may not like their solutions, but at least that gives you and them a place to start. Given some time, your people will appreciate the fact that you have confidence in their ability to solve most problems. This doesn't preclude you from subtly pointing them in the right direction, if in fact you know the right direction. No matter how good you are, you just might not know the answer to every situation. That's why you have a good staff.

What is the main reason for getting them to solve, or at least help solve, problems? Because problem solving should be done at the level of the organization where the problem exists. Why? Because, in many cases, that is the level where there is the most knowledge of the problem and what can be done about it. All too often, upper-level management will come up with a solution, which they of course think is brilliant, and then find out they didn't even have a good handle on the problem, let alone the solution. Why not get the people with the problem to come up with the solution? First, they know more about the real problem than anyone, and second, they probably know the solution, if someone would just listen to them. And if the solution is theirs, they will have much more incentive to make it work.

Example . . .

At one assignment, at a manufacturing
company, the final assembly department
experienced a problem getting the product
out the door. As in the past, the assembly
department was waiting for someone to
come and solve the problem.

The production manager, my direct
report, and I discussed the fact that there
was a problem there and decided to let
the assembly department try and solve it.
The production manager put the burden
of solving the problem on the shoulders
of the assembly department foreman and
whomever he chose to work with him on
a solution. This action caused some drama
until the production manager explained
that we needed solutions and not drama.
After thinking about it, the foreman was
pleased that we showed faith in his ability
to solve the problem. When he got his
people together, they found that pinpointing
the exact problem was not that hard,
and a solution soon came to mind. They
brought the solution and presented it to the
production manager and me, and we gave
them the green light to put the solution in
place. We made sure that the department
people got full credit for coming up with
their own solution. It made them feel

like they could accomplish anything. The reaction through the plant was extremely positive, leading to more departments wanting to solve their own problems.

Now this doesn't mean you can sit back and not take responsibility for problems that need solving. When people come with problems and solutions, you sit and listen, suggest, help direct their thinking, and agree on a solution, help set timetables, and see to follow-up and implementation.

Example . . .

One day, the human resources manager came into my office and explained that employees were having a hard time understanding the finer points of our new healthcare benefits. Their lack of understanding caused unneeded drama in the workplace. Also, it took too much time for her department to keep explaining it to each employee who came in asking questions. I told her to go back to her department and come up with a better way to explain the program. I also suggested that they might want to get the insurance carrier involved in the effort. She went back and soon came up with an excellent solution. They, with the help of the insurance carrier, put together a booklet explaining all the questions being asked by the employees. She distributed the booklet to all employees and gave them out as part of the new hiring process. The demand on her department for answering questions dropped off dramatically.

What do you do if your staff has already left you problems to solve? You meet with staff and gently explain that in reality, they are in the best position to solve or at least come up with solution options, and that you have the utmost confidence they will. Then set a specific time for them to get back to you with those options. You need to do this in such a way that shows you still care if the problem gets solved, and that you are always ready to help them sort out their options, but that the responsibility is on them to take the lead in finding solutions.

If you have chosen someone to solve a problem, and that person ends his or her employment with you, select someone else to solve the problem. Explain to this person what you would like done, and encourage them to look at the problem with a fresh set of eyes.

To summarize: No-drama management suggests that people who come to you with problems, but without solutions in mind, should be sent back to work out possible solutions. Before sending them back, you may need to direct their thinking. Then set a definite time for them to return with suggestions on how to solve the problem.

Of course, some problems will be yours to deal with, and these should be handled with the

same swift no-drama dispatch you expect from
your direct reports.

———

NOTHING WILL HELP EMPOWER YOUR STAFF
MORE THAN LETTING THEM, OR GENTLY
FORCING THEM, TO SOLVE, OR AT LEAST
HELP SOLVE, THEIR PROBLEMS.
AND THEN OF COURSE, MAKE SURE
THEY GET THE CREDIT.

⇥25⇤

Friend or Manager? Pick One

How do you relate to direct reports or others in the company? I've never seen a close friendship between a manager and a direct report, or someone answering to that direct report, be a positive force in the manager's ability to manage. On the contrary, I've seen time and again where such a friendship got in the way of what that manager could do. If it didn't actually influence his or her management decisions everyone around the situation thought it did, so the result was about the same.

So how do you relate to the other people in your company? You are friendly with them at work and when you meet them in a restaurant or supermarket, but you are not their friend. You treat them with respect. You joke with them and maybe tease them or tell a funny story on yourself, but again you're not their friend. If they want to talk, you listen to their non-work related problems, triumphs, and worries. You congratulate them on their children's graduations, marriages, or not-guilty verdicts, but you are not part of their non-working lives. If a decision needs to be made involving that person, you must be able to approach that decision in a no-drama way, with only the company's well-being in mind.

This may sound cold, and many managers can't deal with people that way, but the good managers have or acquire that ability. That doesn't mean you can't empathize with the employees, or see that they get all the support company policy says they should get in whatever situation they find themselves. But I know that being close friends with a fellow employee complicates any decision that has to be made concerning that employee. And whatever decision you make, no one is going to give you credit for making the right one.

Example . . .

> John is a regional sales manager. His boss, the sales vice president, reports to you. Your family spends time with John and his family. He is a good friend and everyone knows it. It comes time to appoint a replacement for the sales vice president. You think John could do the job. But you start thinking about what people are going to think because he's a friend. (If that thought doesn't cross your mind, then you have a

problem understanding how your actions
affect others.) So you choose John for the
position, but only make him acting sales
vice president so people will think you're
not playing favorites. Well, guess what? That
doesn't fool anyone, and in addition, will
stir up a great deal of drama. People are
upset because you obviously picked a friend
instead of the most competent person, or
so they think. John is upset because of the
acting part of his title. He knows he is best
for the position and rightly guesses that you
are afraid of public opinion. John complains
bitterly to his wife who is not speaking to
your wife, who is mad at you for being so
spineless. Get the picture?

Now if people are your friends already, then
you just have to work around and through that.
But for heaven's sake, don't go out and make your
employees your friends, thinking this bonding
will make you a better manager. It always looks
desperate to me for a manager to make friends
with the people he leads for eight hours a day. Find
your friends someplace else.

All of the above is also true of romantic relationships with the same group of people. At the
very least, it will weaken your position, if not get you
fired or accused of sexual harassment. And again, it
will create more drama and wasted energy.

Example . . .

At one assignment, a company department head tried to be friends with all the department's employees. She thought they would do whatever she wanted out of friendship. She went to lunch with them, which is different than taking them out to lunch once in awhile as a reward for hard work or some extra effort. She bought them little gifts and attended their Tupperware parties. She tried to buy their loyalty. When it became necessary for her to deal with them in a way they thought not proper for a friend, everyone got upset. The whole department stayed in a state of turmoil with several ongoing dramas wasting time and energy. I ended up appointing someone else to head up the department; that solved the whole drama problem.

Another example . . .

At another assignment, there was a plant manager who hunted, fished, bowled, and barbequed with his direct reports and some other employees. He was a good technical manager, but these relationships with his people kept getting in the way. People in the department always felt that the best assignments went to his "buddies," but when they actually didn't, the "buddies" got upset. The end result? Continual drama and discontent resulting in substandard productivity. After talking with him about the reason for the turmoil, the plant manager gently moved away from all the togetherness with his employees, and over time, the turmoil and drama evaporated.

Keeping yourself aloof will allow you to treat everyone with the same evenhanded fairness. This doesn't mean that you present a cold, uncaring, or unfriendly personality. You just don't spend time or socialize with employees outside the workplace.

——◦◦◦——

TOO MANY TIMES I'VE SEEN MANAGERS TRY TO BE BOTH FRIEND AND MANAGER TO THOSE WHO REPORTED TO THEM, AND NOT DO WELL AT EITHER.

→26←

When Things Get Better

Possibly one of the most dangerous times for the company is when things start to improve. The general tendency is to relax when you have things running smoothly. Everyone has the feeling that "We've done it!" You have done something, and everyone should be applauded. But "you've only just begun," as a songwriter once suggested. Management should always be on the lookout for things that may be creeping up on them.

The spending of money, for instance, should be done with as much deliberation in good times as in bad. When times get better, you will buy things you wouldn't have bought when things were tough. But do so with the usual thought and deliberation.

Your continuous improvement teams should still be functioning, and you still need to be a part of them, if not leading the deliberations. This is not

117

the time to settle back and let everyone relax.

Example . . .

At one assignment, we turned the corner on getting the company back on its feet and felt pretty confident. The production people came in with an idea for a new piece of equipment that would ostensibly give us multiple advantages, including labor savings and increased profits. Without much thought, we went ahead with this purchase and found ourselves with not only a piece of equipment that wouldn't perform up to our inflated expectations, but also one that didn't fit into what the company was trying to accomplish. We ended up dumping the equipment on someone who thought it would solve his problems and did so at a loss. We had relaxed our vigilance because so many things we undertook turned out well, we thought that trend would miraculously continue.

Example . . .

At another assignment, we pulled the company back from the brink of a Chapter 11 and felt justifiably good. But then we got a little lax. Our manufacturing company distributed to retail stores around the country. We managed one successful self-owned retail outlet. So we thought, why not open another retail store? Without really

determining why the first location was
successful, and without really studying the
market around the possible new location,
and without really having the funds
available, we opened the second location.
It barely broke even, while taking up an
inordinate amount of management's time.
The bottom line: We weren't as careful as we
would have been earlier.

Sound management dictates that the hard
work and due diligence never stop, no matter how
well the company is doing.

—◦◦◦—

NEVER BECOME COMPLACENT AND THINK
THAT SUCCESS WILL AUTOMATICALLY BREED
SUCCESS WITHOUT THE HARD WORK.

→27←

Stay Focused

It is easy to get excited or enamored by some new idea, process, product, or service. If your staff and their people are doing their jobs, they will be coming in with many new ideas about how to improve the company. This is great, as this is what they are supposed to be doing. Everyone should always be thinking about what could be done to improve product offerings, operations, or looking at ways to improve any of the processes.

Every new idea, process, product, or service needs to be measured against what the company is trying to accomplish. Will it improve the company's performance or detract from what the company is trying to do? Will the new idea help the company stay financially healthy and relevant?

As these ideas come in, you will get many opinions on their viability. People presenting or listening to new ideas can easily become dramatic. If they know the ground rules it will eliminate much of the drama. But again, it will be your no-drama management style that will help you and your people stay away from the drama and not let it become the focus of your discussions.

You must have at least a semi-formal way to measure new ideas against the company goals. This can be your continuous improvement team. Everyone should understand what tests any new idea will have to pass before being put into place, the service announced, the money spent, or the time and personnel committed. If the people know this procedure beforehand, they will answer most of the questions before presenting the idea formally. This preparation will give any new idea the best possible chance to be fully heard and eliminate most of the drama that can be generated during these presentations.

There are times when a new idea turns out to be so robust it will change the direction of the company or at least part of the company. If the company has to change direction, do it deliberately and after all possible due diligence. Don't let it happen to you by accident, although that is certainly not unheard of. If the company has its direction changed accidentally, it will more likely go in the wrong direction.

Example . . .

At one assignment, the company produced a large number of short cuts of wood that went into the chippers and then burnt to help supply heat to the complex. It was not a total waste, but several employees recognized it as an opportunity. They developed the idea to take these short pieces of board and develop a cut-stock program. In other words, we could supply other manufacturers with short lengths of board, which was their basic raw material. We priced the product in a very advantageous way for both us and the customer. After due deliberation and making sure it fit into what we were trying to do, we went ahead with the project. Within six months, this new division became the fastest growing portion of the company, with great profit margins.

Don't ashcan all the ideas that come along and can't be immediately used; keep them in a file someplace. The rate of change in business is accelerating and your company goals will evolve. You never know when last year's crazy idea might be just what you need today.

Example . . .

At one assignment, we looked at building a line of bunk beds that used heavier than normal lumber. These bunk beds were heavy looking and sturdy. However, after costing them out and comparing that to the price we could sell them for, we found it just didn't fit into the company's goals.

A couple years later, a small beetle went through our part of the country and killed a certain portion of the pine trees. The result to the trees was that, even though the wood remained sound as long as we harvested the trees soon, the wood became partially discolored, sort of blue actually. Because of the blue color, not much could be done with it in normal lumber or furniture manufacturing. The choices were to let the dead trees rot in the forest or find a use for that timber. These salvaged trees became available at a greatly reduced cost to whoever could use them. That's when we dusted off the previous plan for the heavy bunk beds. We harvested this "blue" pine and made our bunk beds out of it. They were a big hit. Because of the decreased value/cost of this lumber, we were able to show a profit on the new bunk bed line. In fact, we bought "blue" pine from neighboring timber harvesters and used it also. The idea that didn't work at one time turned into a lifesaver later.

The focus should not be on just doing well what you're now doing, but on doing that which will help meet the company's goal of financial strength through profitability, or in the case of a not-for-profit organization, enhance your service. If what you are doing or proposing doesn't further the company toward those goals, then change.

—~~~—

Establish goals for the company, and then measure all proposals and performance against those goals.

→28←

Do With What You've Got

During a crisis situation, where time is of the essence and you lack resources, it is easy to fall into the "if we only had this" trap. "If we had the time and money, we could buy in better economic quantities, we could develop a new line, we could buy that new piece of equipment, etc, we could poll the customers and see what they really want, we could do a lot of things that we can't do because we don't have the resources." It is easy to fall into that trap. But if there was ever a time for innovative thinking, it is now.

Get your team thinking of ways to accomplish the same things without the benefit of the resources you at first think you might need.

Example . . .

In the early days of each assignment, when we were struggling to get each

company back on its feet, I found myself
continually saying, "We'll have to make
those delivery trucks last another six
months," or "Let's refurbish that machine
and make it last another year," or "We've
got as much going to advertising as we
can afford already." You get the picture.
But when saying "no," I also shared enough
financial information with the supplicants so
they could clearly understand why.

Example . . .

At one assignment, where I became
involved after a Chapter 11 went into
effect, the vendors became understandably
reluctant to sell supplies to the company
on credit. But we didn't have the money to
pay cash, so we were at a stalemate. Without
supplies we couldn't make the product to
pay for the supplies. So after developing a
business plan, we met separately with the
vendors, and without any drama, explained
what we would be doing and how we
meant to do it. We promised to give them
a monthly update on our progress in cash
flow and sales progress. We convinced the
vendors to sell to us on credit, thereby
letting us move ahead with production and
sales. This would not be called world-class
innovation, but it certainly was not business
as usual.

Example . . .

At another assignment, we desperately needed a new planer/sander. We didn't have the funds to buy one on normal terms nor, because of our shaky financial situation, could we lease one. We knew which vendor we wanted to do business with, so we brought in that vendor, sat him down, explained our situation in a professional way. Again we laid out our business plan and what we hoped to accomplish. We also let him talk with the people who would be operating and maintaining the new sander to make him comfortable with our technical expertise. We worked out a deal whereby he let us use a new planer/sander he developed and wanted to debug in a real time situation. We came to an agreement on terms and conditions that both parties felt comfortable with, and it worked out fine.

In both these situations we knew what we needed, what we intended doing if we got it, and what we hoped to accomplish in the long term. We remained completely honest about our financial situation. Our no-drama professionalism was a great plus also.

What I'm saying is this: in a crisis situation explore every idea and solicit those ideas from every quarter.

—◦◦◦—

USE ALL THE INNOVATION AVAILABLE IN
OR OUT OF YOUR COMPANY TO GET
THE MOST OUT OF YOUR RESOURCES.

❖29❖

Computers & Software— Heaven Help Us All

Let me say a word about computers and computer software—probably the biggest inventions since the pizza. With them, we can send spaceships to explore Mars, photograph Jupiter, or print and catalog our pictures. I use computers extensively and wouldn't know what to do without one. If I tried to do all my personal projects on paper, it would bury me, so the computer is a great tool, right? Right!

But hold on a minute. Now keep in mind I'm not speaking of computerized production equipment here, which covers anything from the PC that helps with word processing to CAD software that multiplies the effectiveness of an engineer or architect. I'm talking about computers helping with business systems: for example, order maintenance, order tracking, manufacturing scheduling, and materials and inventory management, just to name a few.

There can be a tendency to want to bring computer sophistication to bear on workplace problems when the problems are caused by inefficiency, the lack of organization, or the lack of well-thought-out processes. The usual result, along with much drama if not managed, will be lack of efficiency and organization at a higher rate of speed. Many of your people will look at the results, and because they're being spit out of a computer, take it as gospel. The smart ones will either try to fix the system, or they will keep enough information on the side so they can function. The old adage of garbage in, garbage out is still applicable.

Example . . .

At one assignment, the company received and processed dozens of complex orders every day. Any given order needed to be broken down to its several manufacturing departments, then broken down again to the individual components. A simple order could generate 1,000 line items to be filed, pulled up, tracked, and all brought together at the right time for assembly, shipping, and billing. Over the years the company developed a good paperwork system, but we could see that as our volume kept growing, the job of maintaining this system would get to be labor intensive. So we decided to commit the resources to developing a computerized system that would do everything we did on paper. We knew exactly what we wanted the computer to do as we were already doing most of it by hand. We knew our current costs to work this system, so it was easy to figure the payback on the resources needed to develop the new system. Once the system was in place, it did exactly what we wanted, with a little less labor, and the process did not take much additional labor as the volume increased. An added bonus was that with the additional information at our fingertips, we were able to utilize to good effect this readily available information for better management of the company.

Example . . .

We experienced a problem keeping an inventory of what we actually needed to build the product we had on order. A major disconnect existed between incoming orders, purchasing, and inventory control. We just couldn't seem to get a handle on the situation. We met our shipping dates, but it was a hard, awkward process. Once again, a great deal of information needed to be considered for each order as the product was all custom-made. Of course, the first idea that came to mind involved our buying or developing software to handle all this divergent data. We became convinced that plan of action would solve our problems.

So the search began. We looked at the

possibilities of either outsourcing the
software or developing it in-house. We really
didn't have a clear idea of just what the
process should be, or how it would work
best, always a dangerous position to be in.
The sessions to make this decision involved
considerable drama, as everyone possessed
a strong opinion of what we should do
and what software might be best. But we
realized that drama was only a way to slow
down the process and we avoided it as much
as possible.

We finally decided to purchase a software
package that promised the moon, realizing
we would have to modify it to fit our
particular situation. In the middle of this
project, I moved on to another assignment,
but kept track of this particular effort to
see how it would work itself out. It never
did. After struggling for several years with
the very expensive software and trying
to modify it to the company's needs, the
company finally just bagged the whole
project.

If you have a situation where the system
is running smoothly and efficiently, then computerizing it just might, and probably will, speed
up the process, and even eliminate the need to hire
more help in the future as your business grows.

I've never seen a situation where computerizing
a system saved much labor at the onset, although

every presentation promised to do just that. But I've seen the computer curtail the need for bringing in more people in the future to handle growth.

All I'm trying to say is that when a direct report comes in all out of breath and tells you that computerizing the big mess they have in customer service, manufacturing, shipping, or wherever will solve everything, be extremely wary.

—◈◈◈—

LOOK TWICE BEFORE LEAPING INTO COMMITTING RESOURCES ON COMPUTERIZING SYSTEMS OR PROCESSES.

⇥30⇤

Think Ahead

Part of your no-drama management will be to keep your team at least partially focused on the future of the company and not just the current fires, even during a crisis situation.

At such a time, you still need to be working on long-range plans. Employees need to see this and be a part of it. For one thing, long-range plans give everyone confidence that there is going to be a future to put those plans into effect. During a crisis, it's easy to get bogged down in the drama of the daily fires you need to put out, but everyone should be working on ways to prevent fires in the future.

Example . . .

> At one assignment, we experienced times when we weren't sure we were going to be able to make the next payroll, but we still worked on continuous improvement and long-range plans as if we had all the time

and money in the world. As we survived each succeeding week, these continuous improvements started to take effect, and we finally got the company in a position where making the next payroll was no longer any kind of problem.

But I know it's very easy to get into this fire-fighting mode during a crisis. To overcome this, as each fire is put out, sit down with the people involved and decide what to do so that particular fire does not repeat itself. As the expression goes "Don't keep fighting the alligators; drain the swamp."

Keep in mind that long-range plans are never exact, and will be based on a number of assumptions. Because of this, these plans will need to be reviewed and probably changed, or at least updated on a regular basis.

—◦◦◦—

DON'T LET A CURRENT CRISIS PREVENT
YOU FROM THINKING AHEAD.

→31←

120 Over 80

The management situation you might be considering or are already engaged in can be very stressful. We are told that stress can be a killer. Of course in this day and age, we hear that about everything—pizza, eggs, milk, salt, and I'm sure you have your favorites. But even if stress does not kill, it can make life unpleasant for you and those around you, so why not learn to handle it, or at least minimize the results? You know, take the edge off the stress. You can buy numerous books telling you how to do this: for example, exercise, diet, talk to your plants, watch your fish swim around, and so forth.

Why do something about the stress? Because, unless resolved, it will have a debilitating physical and mental effect on your ability to provide sound no-drama management.

There are a few things that will, in my opinion, help you manage stress. At least they work for me.

Physical activity helps me lower stress levels, whether it's mowing the lawn, walking around the factory floor, or climbing the stairs instead of taking the elevator. But physical activity doesn't get to the cause of the stress.

Being a no-drama manager will limit stress as it will cut down the number of stressful encounters you have to deal with.

Be Proactive—Do something about the cause. First, you have to figure out just what is bothering you. Sit down and ask yourself, just what bothers me about this situation? Why am I feeling stressed? Many times, by defining the uneasy or scared feeling you have, it dissolves into a non-problem.

Ask yourself:

♦ Am I stressed from fear of failure?
♦ Am I stressed from fear of something physical, like falling into the chipper, getting beat-up by the creditors, or becoming sick or disabled?
♦ Am I stressed from fear of what people will think?
♦ Am I stressed because I don't know what to do?

For me, once I've defined the thing causing me stress, most of the stress just goes away.

Why? Because I find that:

♦ I can't control the problem I'm worrying about.

♦ I can do something about the situation by putting a plan into action.

If I imagine the worst possible outcome, will I still have:

♦ My life?
♦ My family?
♦ My health?
♦ My ability to continue functioning?

Ninety-nine percent of the time, the answer is yes, and I ask myself, "Then why are you stressing about it?"

As I said, this works for me, and I hope it will help you in the stressful situations you will have if you are in a management position.

Keep in mind that a little stress can be exhilarating, keep you on your toes, and provide just enough adrenalin to make life interesting.

———

ONCE THE CAUSATIVE FACTORS
OF STRESS ARE OUT IN THE OPEN
THEY DON'T SEEM NEARLY AS SCARY.

⇥32⇤

Don't Burn Bridges

Unless you're clairvoyant it's usually best not to burn bridges. Don't cut off a person or a company because you have no use for them now or because of some disagreement. The problem with burning bridges is you may have a need for the person or company in the future.

Example . . .

At one of my assignments, we were assigned a new vendor's rep who called on us to sell and service his company's commodity-type product, which we used on a regular basis. This guy turned out to be a first-class jerk. His being opinionated, prejudiced and vocal about everything didn't help make him any more acceptable. We could have gotten this product from several sources, but after dealing with this particular company for many years we decided not to sever the relationship. After he first started calling on us, our purchasing manager came into my office after each visit just boiling. She wanted to bar the guy from ever coming back on the property. However, being an intelligent lady, she realized that burning bridges was probably not what we really wanted to do. In short order everyone got used to him, unfortunately, and he just became a joke.

One day, this rep showed up with a trainee in tow. The purchasing manager brought the two of them to my office. The rep didn't introduce the trainee or include her in any of the conversation. I finally introduced myself. The only time he acknowledged the trainee was to make a disparaging remark about her earrings. When we tried to ask her questions or include her in any way, the rep butted in and cut her off. His performance embarrassed everyone except himself. As they left my office, I found myself next to the trainee, so I leaned over and quietly said, "I like your earrings." It was a small gesture. After about a month, this trainee replaced our jerk of a rep. And she made an exceptional sales rep. Any time her company had some special pricing or inventory closeouts, we were the first to be called. She went out of her way to take care of us, and when asked about it, she made no bones about the fact that it stemmed from the fact that we liked her earrings. Every once in a while she would stick her head in

my office and laughingly ask if I liked her
new ear jewelry. Now the easy thing would
have been to tell the jerk of a rep to clear off
and for us to buy our product from someone
else, but by not doing that, we profited in
the long run.

Keep in mind that I'm not talking about ever
accepting poor quality or poor service. That would
be a completely different situation. If you are in a
situation where you just cannot use a company's
product or services any longer because of poor
quality or service, sit them down and tell them why
you have decided to buy elsewhere. Let them know
if they get their problems sorted out to please come
back and talk to you.

Example . . .

Someone had offered one of my good
managers employment and he came into my
office to say his goodbyes. His leaving would
inconvenience the company and possibly
affect its profits. Was this the time to tell
this person what I thought of his leaving me
in the lurch, making it harder to do my job,
and possibly setting a bad example to other
employees? No way. I was not going to burn
the bridge to this employee's possible return.

I congratulated him on his good fortune
and wished him all the best in the new
endeavor. I also assured him that if he ever
needed a job, he should contact me. I didn't

say more than that. I didn't promise him a
job, but just let him know I would certainly
consider him if the occasion ever came
up. The employee left with a good feeling
toward the company. He knew that he had
a fall-back position. The worst that could
have happened? This employee would
remember me and the company in a kind
way and would reflect those feelings when
talking with other people. The best that
could happen? We would get this employee
back some day, or at least the chance of first
refusal.

Another example . . .

At another assignment, we were selling
to a particular customer whose absentee
owners suddenly announced a Chapter 7
bankruptcy and disappeared while owing
us considerable money. It would have been
enjoyable to yell and rant at the manager
of this business, since he was the only one
we could get our hands on. While we didn't
invite him over for meatloaf, neither did we
endeavor to go out of our way to give him
a bad time over the situation. That turned
out to be a good thing as he soon moved to
another larger firm, and started ordering and
paying for our product, thus giving us the
opportunity to recoup our original loss.

Burning bridges is usually about self-gratification. And I've never seen a case where indulging in self-gratification improved a person's ability to be a better manager.

—◆◆◆—

REMEMBER: YOU CAN SEVER RELATIONSHIPS THAT ARE BAD FOR THE COMPANY, WHILE LEAVING THE POSSIBILITY FOR WORKING TOGETHER IN THE FUTURE.

⋙33⋘

Enjoy!

Working takes up at least one-third of our time, and if you are a manager probably more than that. Good managers will be so excited about what they are doing that they think about their work while behind the wheel, in the shower, and almost any other place. Therefore, they will spend probably up to half of their time at, or thinking about, work.

In my opinion, work is a blessing, maybe a mixed blessing, but a blessing nonetheless. Not many people are so economically disadvantaged that they don't have to work, or at least want to work, if for no other reason than to buy food, shelter, and other of life's necessities.

Many people feel that they HAVE to go to work! It is your job to, if not to make the other employees want to come to work, to at least make them feel good about what they are accomplishing. This in turn will make you feel good about what you are doing. This is what practicing sound no-drama management will do for you.

So considering how much time you as a manager will spend working, why shouldn't it be enjoyable?

Webster defines work as follows: "Effort exerted to do or make something." You as a manager are making something, and that is a better department, company, or organization. And the biggest thing you're making is yourself and your staff into better no-drama managers.

There will certainly be times when your work is more enjoyable than at other times, but on the average it should be enjoyable, something you look forward to, something that makes you glad when the weekend is over and you can get back to being an above average manager, directing your department or company into becoming better and better.

If it's not enjoyable, then maybe you are doing the wrong thing, either at work or in life in general, or approaching your work or life with an attitude that precludes you from enjoying what you're doing. You might be taking yourself too seriously.

Try to see the humor in what you are doing and what happens around you. Laugh at that humor and laugh at yourself. Get your direct reports to see the humor around them. One good way to help yourself enjoy what you're doing is to help others around you enjoy what they are doing.

The last example, I promise . . .

At all my assignments, I told my people early on that if we couldn't have fun doing what we were doing, or going to do, then we were probably in the wrong place. And sure enough, we did. Not every single moment of every day, but in general, it was a fun time.

There are some people who just cannot enjoy themselves while in a stressful situation. It's your job to help them enjoy themselves, or suggest to them that they might want to find something they can enjoy, because . . .

———〰———

LIFE IS JUST TOO SHORT
NOT TO ENJOY WHAT YOU'RE DOING!

About the Author

Eldon Spady has spent his career managing departments and divisions as well as entire companies. He has held positions as department manager, vice president, executive vice president, general manager, and president. A number of the companies he was engaged to manage were either in Chapter 11 or on the brink of liquidation and/or Chapter 13 bankruptcy. The causes of their troubles ran the gamut from lack of funds to dysfunctional management. With the exception of one, all these companies, whose annual revenues ranged from seven million to sixty-five million dollars, were turned around under his guidance and are alive and well today. Mr. Spady brings to the table a vast repertoire of knowledge and skills which includes Profit & Loss Management, Operational Analysis, Troubleshooting, and most important of all, Team Building.

Printed in Great Britain
by Amazon